A second level beginners book that will help you turn the tables and take charge of your IBM PC or compatible computer

by Peter Harrison

**First Edition - May 1991**



We wish to thank the following for their contributions:

*Peter Harrison, PC Productions Ltd*, manuscript
*Epps Ransom Associates*, London, cover design
*Studio Etyd AB*, Sweden, cover picture
*Prometheus design*, Sweden, cartoons & artwork
*BPCC Hazell Books Ltd*, Aylesbury, printing

**PC Productions Ltd**
**Kendrick Hall**
**Kendrick Street**
**Stroud**
**Glos. GL5 1AA**
**U.K.**

**Tel: 0453-755200**
**Fax: 0453-755400**
**InterMail: 0453-755600**

ISBN 1 873005 01 6

# Preface

**Welcome to PC Crash Course II!**

**PC Crash Course II** is a second level beginners book about PCs. It is a follow-up to the world-wide success **PC Crash Course and Survival Guide.** If you have already grasped the absolute basics of computing, but still feel that there is a lot left that needs explaining, then this is the book for you.

**PC Crash Course II** will help you to learn more about computers in two ways. Firstly it is packed with easy explanations of computers and their workings, filling in many vital gaps in your knowledge of PCs. Secondly it covers many of the most common problems that you will be faced with like strange printouts, keyboard problems, memory expansion and viruses, to name just a few. By absorbing the suggestions on how to tackle these problems you will acquire an all-round knowledge of your PC.

Quite simply, **PC Crash Course II** will help you to turn the tables and take charge!

Peter Harrison.

## About this book

This book is divided into eight chapters, and also contains four useful appendices. Even if you don't already own a computer, you can derive a lot of benefit from reading this book. Reading it is an excellent way to prepare yourself for talking to computer sales persons, or "techies" in your office, since after going through it you'll know more than the basics needed to converse intelligently with them.

The following topics are covered in this book:

**1. More About Computers**

A glossary of computer terms that will help you to get the most out of this book. It takes you much further than the topics covered in the first book in this series

- **PC Crash Course & Survival Guide** - and will expand and enhance your general computer knowledge.

**2. Batch Files and AUTOEXEC.BAT**

Explains what a batch file is and teaches you how to write your own. The all-important AUTOEXEC.BAT file is also covered. Many example batch files are given helping you to understand the available batch file commands.

**3. Memory - Organisation and Expansion**

Explains all about computer memory and its organisation and the effects DOS and memory resident programs have on it. You can read how to expand your computer's memory with conventional, extended or expanded memory.

**4. Diskettes and Drives**

Here diskettes and diskette drives are covered in detail. You can also read about problems arising from having different types of diskettes and drives and about everything you need to know about formatting different diskettes. The DOS command ASSIGN is also covered.

**5. Hard Disks** Gives many practical details on hard disks and the problems that may arise including fragmentation and optimization. Furthermore you can read about the 32 Mb limit and the different standards that are used.

**6. Printers** This chapter explains how different printers work and goes through some of the most common problems a printer can cause. Installation via parallel or serial ports is discussed, as is the DOS command MODE. You can also read about how control codes affect the printout.

**7. Keyboards, Mice and Other Input Devices**

Teaches you about your keyboard and discusses the problems you may meet. Covers installing and using a mouse and discusses other input devices.

**8. Danger - Computer Virus at Large**

Discusses the very real threat of computer viruses, giving many examples of known viruses and how to detect them. You can find out a few simple ways to protect your computer against a total breakdown.

The appendices cover the following topics:

**Appendix A. The ASCII and PostScript Character Sets**

**Appendix B. Some Example Formatting Batch Files**

**Appendix C. Some Common DOS Error Messages**

**Appendix D. Some Useful DOS Commands**

# Different typefaces used

To make it easier for you to read and understand this manual, we have used different typefaces as follows:

Items that you are to type on the keyboard are printed in colour and in a different typeface:

`do this`

Items that appear on the screen are printed in a different typeface, and are boxed in, as shown below:

```
Screen display
```

Items which refer to something displayed on your screen are shown as follows:

`This refers to something shown on your screen.`

Whenever we refer to specific keys, we print either the symbol, or the keyname as follows:

↵

or

**Home**

You should be aware that screen displays shown in this book are only examples, and frequently will differ from those that are displayed on your screen. This isn't our fault or - more importantly - yours. There are literally thousands of different combinations of computer parts and operating systems that all are considered part of the IBM-PC family of computers and clones, and each does things just a little bit differently.

# Table of Contents

# 1. More About Computers

This chapter presents a glossary of selected computer terms. It is the very least you should know about computers to gain full benefit from this book. If you are relatively new to computers it should be an invaluable start - confirming the knowledge you already have and enhancing it with explanations of other basic and important ideas. If you already know quite a lot about computers, then you will not need to read all of this chapter, but may still be able to fill in some gaps in your knowledge.

Many of the terms have been dealt with thoroughly in the first book in this series, **PC Crash Course and Survival Guide**. Other terms will be covered in full later on in this book.

The terms are not presented in alphabetical order as it is not meant to be a look-up reference - they are divided into logically related sections as follows:

- Hardware units
  Computer basics
  Information storage
  Other add-ons
  DOS (Disk Operating System)
  Application programs
  Communications
  Networks
  Programming
  Other terms

Finally, please remember that the glossary does not intend to give an exhaustive explanation of each term, which would thoroughly exhaust you as well, but is meant to provide a concise and accurate description using language that is easy to understand. It is also assumed that you are not a complete and absolute beginner, in which case you are recommended to read the afore mentioned book - **PC Crash Course and Survival Guide**.

## Hardware units

When running through the basics of computers and computing, it seems reasonable to start with the physical units that you have on the table in front of you, as these are the most obvious parts - to use a computer you need a method of passing data to the computer (e.g. via the keyboard) and a method of seeing the results (i.e. on the screen or a printout).

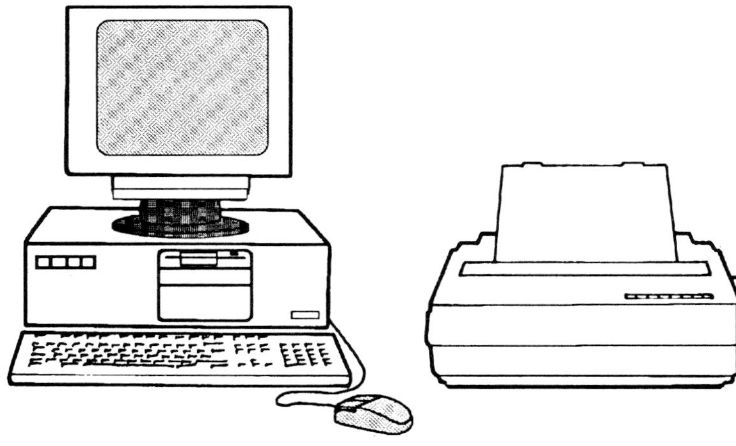

## CPU

The CPU (Central Processing Unit), or System unit as it is sometimes known, houses several main parts of a computer. As well as the power unit, it also contains the central processor, the computer's memory (ROM and RAM) and the storage units (hard disk and diskette drives), all of which are explained later on in this chapter.

CPU's always used to be placed on your table, and the screen fitted nicely on top. These days, so-called tower models, which stand on the floor, are becoming more and more common. Your desk becomes less cluttered, the disturbing noise is pushed under the table and the screen ends up where... on the desk, which is definitely too low for a comfortable sitting position, and you need to find an ugly cardboard box to put it on (perhaps you have a delightful velvet cloth to hide it under!), or you just have to put a £100 swivel arm monitor stand on your list of Christmas presents and hope that someone is feeling charitable.

Most computer models are available as a tower model or as an old-fashioned desk top model. If you change to a tower model think about the screen first!

## Keyboard

The keyboard is used (obviously!) to type in information, numbers and words, to make selections from menus, to move the cursor and to give commands. A whole chapter of this book is devoted to the keyboard and other input devices, and the problems that can arise with them.

## Mouse

A mouse is a pointing object that can be used instead of, or in conjunction with the keyboard. It is particularly useful, and even necessary, when drawing with the computer, or creating printed matter (Desktop Publishing).

When you move the mouse across the table, a rubber ball on the underside of the mouse is rolled around, and its movement converted and conveyed to a pointer on the screen, which is moved in the same way as when you move the cursor with the cursor keys.

A more recent development, the trackball, is rather like an upside down mouse, where you use the palm of your hand to move the ball in the desired direction.

Optical mice also exist. In this case a light sensitive "eye" is moved around on a chequered mat.

There are of course different standards as far as mice are concerned and many mice can perform in different modes. However, all software that uses a mouse is compatible with a Microsoft mouse, so when choosing a mouse always make sure that it has a Microsoft mouse mode.

## Screen

The screen is necessary for the computer to display its results, calculations, graphs, letters, etc. Information is fed to the screen via a graphics card, and that is where the fun starts. There are many standards and each screen needs a suitable graphics card and vice versa. It is no use just buying a colour screen and thinking you automatically will get a colour display.

There are two factors that define the type of screen and graphics card you have. Firstly it is either a colour screen or a monochrome (i.e black and white, or amber/black or green/black). Secondly the resolution of the screen decides the quality of the picture that can be displayed. Each screen has a number of dots, or pixels, that can be illuminated and it is this configuration (e.g. 640 x 320 pixels) that is quoted on sales brochures and adverts, etc.

All screens can display a basic monochrome text display with 25 lines of 80 characters each. Most screens are capable of displaying one or more of the following graphics standards:

| Type | Colour | Pixels |
|---|---|---|
| MDA | No | No graphics |
| HGA (Hercules) | No | 740 x 380 |
| CGA | Yes | 320 x 200 |
| EGA | Yes | 640 x 350 |
| VGA | Yes | 640 x 480 |
| Super VGA | Yes | 800 x 600 |
| UGA | Yes | 1280 x 1024 |

This list is by no means exhaustive and several graphics cards and screens are capable of displaying several standards, and each standard has its own variations. VGA which is becoming the most common standard has, for example, a monochrome mode where grey shades can be displayed, as well as the standard full colour mode.

To complicate the matter even more, all is not dependent on the graphics card and screen. Some programs will only work in certain graphic modes. This is true of much of the free software available that uses graphics and works only with CGA graphics. All the more expensive professional programs, however, can be installed to work with virtually all types of graphics screens with the possible exception of CGA.

A useful type of screen is a Multisync screen that can automatically swap to the graphic standard used by the program.

Most screens are digital screens. That means that each dot, or pixel, can be turned on or off. A grey colour is achieved by a group of pixels working together - the more pixels that are turned off, the darker the grey colour appears. Analogue screens are now becoming more popular for the higher resolutions that VGA provides. With an analogue screen, each dot can be turned on with differing intensities, allowing a wide variety of colours and hues to be displayed. Indeed, the picture quality of super VGA graphics on an analogue screen is impressive.

The standard screen size is 12" to 14", but large screens exist for special purposes. Technical drawings and production of books and documents often benefit from a 20" screen.

Finally, you may wonder why you cannot use your TV set, after all it has a wonderful colour picture. Well, it is not that far away. The 90's will see a lot of computers using the colour TV at home. Several add-in cards already exist that allow you to connect your computer to your TV and video, and transfer pictures to and from your computer.

### Printers

While a printer is not one of the basic and necessary units of a computer system, it is certainly the most common accessory. The aim of most computing is still to produce a printed result.

There are, of course, several different types of printer, all of which are covered, together with printer problems, in a separate chapter later on in the book. Here is a quick reference table:

| Type | Price | Quality | Remarks |
|---|---|---|---|
| Daisy Wheel | Low | High | No graphics |
| Matrix (9 pin) | Low | Low | Poor graphics |
| Matrix (24 pin) | Low-Med | Medium | |
| Ink Jet | Medium | Good-High | |
| Laser | Medium | High | |
| PostScript Laser | High | High | |

There are a few important standards as far as printers are concerned. They are: IBM Proprinter/Graphics for matrix printouts of texts and graphics, Epson FX for matrix printouts of graphics, HP Laser Jet and Postscript for laser printers (texts and graphics). Don't be fooled by an impressive list of emulations that a printer can manage, see to it that it includes one or more of the those mentioned.

### Portables

Portables or Laptops are computers that you can carry around with you so that you can always work even when travelling. Basically you can buy a portable that matches any normal computer but costs more.

The things to watch out for are:

- The screen, check the quality of the display especially if you intend to do a lot of work on it.
- The power supply - does it run on batteries and how long? Some portables need a mains supply, which is a bit of a joke really as you often cannot use them when you most need them.
- The size and weight. Is it really a portable or just a small computer. Excess kilos get very tiresome after a surprisingly short while!

## Computer basics

In this section we will get down to the nitty gritty of the internal workings of a computer. Once again you will not find exhaustive technical explanations, but rather a few basic facts covering the most important aspects.

## Processor

The processor is the brain of the computer. It is here that all data is assessed and all instructions and calculations are carried out.

The type of processor used is what gives the computer its name. You will no doubt have heard of at least some of the terms 8086, 8088, 80286, 80386, 80386SX, 80486, 80586.

The first computers called PC's and XT's had 8086 or 8088 processors, then came the AT's with their 80286 processors. Today 386 machines, with 80386 processors, are becoming more and more common, but the 486s are the state of the art machines. 586s will soon turn up.

Basically each new processor in the chain provides more computing power. The speed at which a computer system operates is governed by many factors, the main one being the clock speed, that is the rate at which the processor is tuned to work.

Here are some common clock speeds given in MHz:

| Processor | Typical clock speeds |
|---|---|
| 8086, 8088 | 4.77, 10 |
| 80286 | 10, 12, 16, 20, 25 |
| 80386 | 16, 20, 25, 33 |
| 80386SX | 16, 20, 25 |
| 80486 | 25, 33 |

Clock speed is just one aspect affecting the overall speed of a system. A 80386 based system running at 33 MHz is typically only half as fast as a 80486 system running at a mere 25 MHz.

A major breakthrough came with the arrival of the 80386 based computers. These could run several programs at the same time, called multitasking, and simply swap between the programs with a few key strokes. A special program is, however, required to achieve this, the most popular being Windows and DesqView 386.

To bring the price of a 386 computer down a special version of the 80386 processor, the 80386SX, was developed. This is a sort of reduced version of the 80386 running at the lower end of the 80386 clock speeds. You may be wondering what you lose out on with a 386SX. The answer is speed alone - a 386SX is in fact one and the same processor as an ordinary 386, but with fewer of its pins connected - it would have been too expensive to develop a new processor for the job.

## Bits and bytes

Bits and bytes are the actual units of memory. One byte is one unit of memory, a letter or a number. Each byte consists of 8 bits which can take the value of 0 or 1. The combination of 0's and 1's determines which character a byte of information represents.

1024 bytes of memory is the same as 1 kilobyte (kb). Thus a computer with 640 kb RAM has in effect 1024 x 640 = 65536 bytes or units of memory each capable of storing 1 character.

A 360 kb diskette can store just over 360000 characters, or around 200 pages of text.

## Memory

The computer's memory is used to store information. There are two sorts of memory ROM and RAM both briefly described below. Memory is also a topic discussed further on in more detail.

## ROM

ROM stands for Read Only Memory. It is a pre-programmed memory chip containing vital information for the computer to function. Read Only means that the data stored can only be read and not changed.

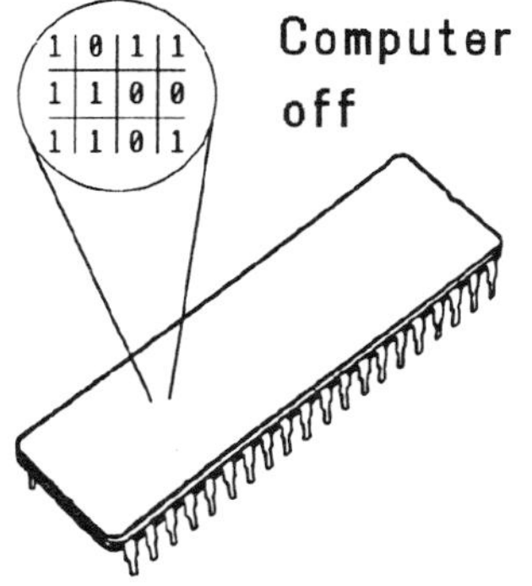


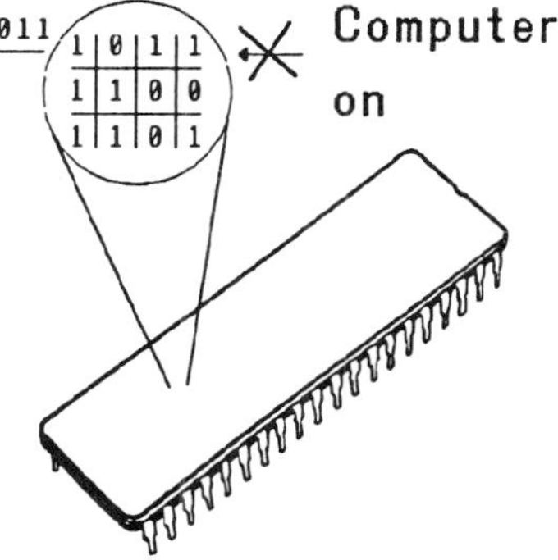

### RAM

RAM stands for Random Access Memory. It is a volatile memory, that is it can store data, have the data wiped out and store new data. It is dependant on a current, so when you switch off the computer the contents of RAM memory disappears.

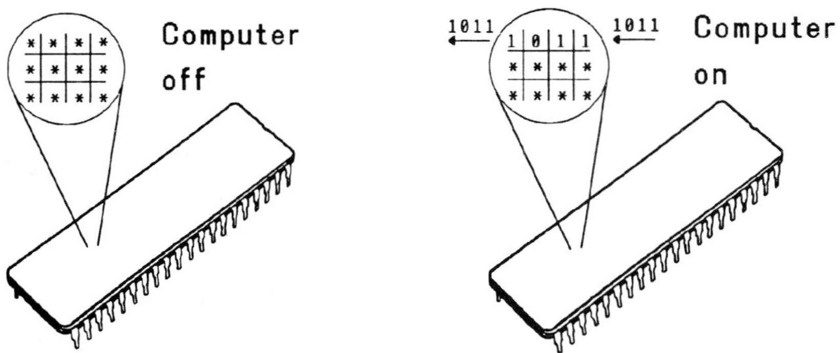


RAM memory is also a measure of how much internal memory your computer has to work with.

## Information storage

Another basic function of a computer is to store data for later retrieval. There are several units on which data can be stored as described briefly here.

### Diskettes and Disk Drives

The diskette is one of the absolute basics of a computer system. There are two sizes - 3.5" and 5.25" - and each size has two types, standard diskettes (often denoted DD, or double density) and high density diskettes. Basically the high density diskettes (HD) can store much more information. The following table shows the storage capacities of these diskettes:

| Type | Storage capacity |
|---|---|
| 3.5" DD | 720 kb |
| 3.5" HD | 1440 kb (1.44 Mb) |
| 5.25" DD | 360 kb |
| 5.25" HD | 1200 kb (1.2 Mb) |

The 5.25" is in fact the old standard and will slowly, very slowly die out. 3.5" diskettes are taking over as they can store more information and are encased in a hard plastic casing thus better protecting your information.

Having two standards does present problems. When buying software you should check that you get the right size of diskette. Later on in this book you will find a chapter that covers diskettes, including the problems that may arise due to this dual standard.

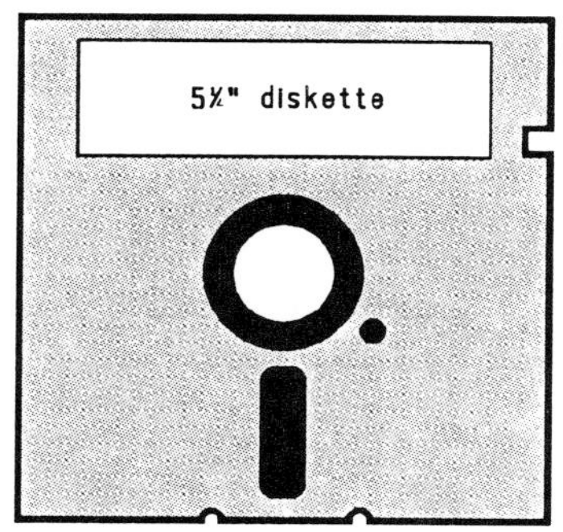

## Hard disks

Hard disks are a vast improvement on diskettes. They can store much much more information, and access it quicker. A few years ago hard disks with 10 Mb (10 000 000 bytes) or 20 Mb storage were considered to be very large. Nowadays a 20 Mb hard disk is only suitable for a home computer, and 10 Mb hard disks are no longer manufactured.

Today we buy hard disks with storage capacities of 30 Mb, 40 Mb, 70 Mb, 100 Mb and even up to 700 Mb. The reason is that more and more programs are arriving and taking up a lot more space on a hard disk.

Some programs can occupy up to 2 Mb storage space so you can see that a 10 Mb hard disk would soon be filled.

There is one danger with larger and larger hard disks - a hard disk crash (failure) can present enormous problems.

## Back-up tape

Anyone working with important information should consider it necessary to take back-up copies of their work. This should be done at regular intervals - even daily for companies with large amounts of information being processed.

The cheapest way of backing up your work is with the help of the DOS command BACKUP, or with a special back-up program, by copying your files onto diskettes. If you have small amounts of work to back up this is fine. Anyone who has done this knows that backing up a 40 Mb hard disk even onces a week becomes a tedious job.

Special back up tape units can be bought and programmed to take back-ups automatically, for example during your lunch hour. The £500 plus investment becomes well worthwhile for anyone with serious amounts of data to back up.

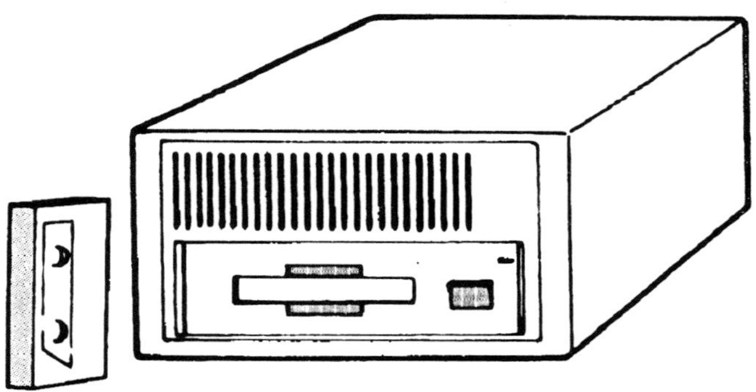

Most people get round to thinking about back-ups when it is already too late. A hard disk crash, or just several important files destroyed or even accidently erased - it is too late. Be wise and think about your needs now.

### CD ROM and WORM

CD ROM is destined to take over as a mass storage medium. CD stands for compact disk and is exactly the same as the musical CD records. In fact a CD ROM drive fitted to your computer can also play music!

The big advantage is the massive storage possibility - 600 Mb on one disk. Perfect for picture libraries, encyclopedias, spelling checkers in several languages, collections of handbooks, library systems, etc. All of these applications already exist in reality.

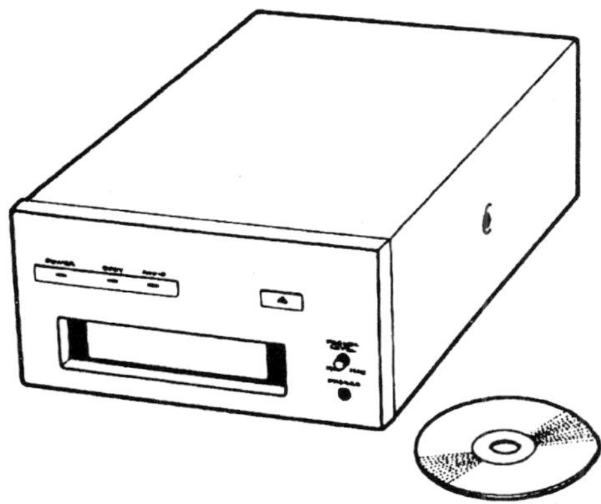

As the name suggests, CD ROM is a read only system. You buy a pre-programmed diskette and cannot change the data on it. This is a major drawback but a WORM technique is being developed. WORM stands for Write Once Read Many. This means you buy an empty disk and can save data on it once, this data becoming permanently etched onto the disk.

## Other add-ons

In this section you can read about some of the most common and most exciting add-on accessories available on the market.

### Scanners and OCR

A scanner is a unit, rather like a camera, that can read a picture into your computer. The picture can then be edited, if you wish, and used in documents and publications. Black and white scanners are the most common sort at the moment, but colour scanners copying full colour pictures into your computer have started to be available.

The result of scanning in something is always a picture. Even if you scan in text the result is a picture and not a text file that you can edit. It is simply a copy of what you see. OCR is a special software designed to recognise text in a scanned picture. Thus a scanner working in conjunction with an OCR program can scan in text and produce a text file that you can then edit.

An OCR program is often just as expensive as the scanner itself. Furthermore OCR programs cannot automatically recognise all text fonts in all sizes. Even line spacing can affect the results. Most OCR programs have been pre-programmed to recognise certain types of print, but can be trained to recognise more.

### Fax card

Sending messages by fax has become a very common and easy method of communication. It is now possible to buy add-in cards that can be connected to your telephone line so that your computer can send and receive fax messages.

### Video grabber

A video grabber allows your computer to grab, or copy pictures from a video camera, video recorder or television set. The pictures can then be edited if necessary and used in other applications.

### Midi interface

Music has long been a neglected feature on the PC simply because the PC system is not really set up to produce more than the odd beep. However, buy connecting a Midi interface and together with a suitable program, your computer can control several musical instruments, and even be used to compose music.

# DOS (Disk Operating System)

DOS is a collection of small programs that enable you to use your computer to store and retrieve information. Without DOS you will not even get your computer started.

Certain DOS features are covered more thoroughly in this book. The most basic commands were covered in the first book, PC Crash Course and Survival Guide, and are not therefore explained fully here. At the end of the book there is an appendix covering the most common DOS commands.

### Internal commands

Internal DOS commands are commands that are always readily available in your computer's memory. They are the most common commands, and are automatically loaded into memory when the computer is started.

### External commands

External DOS commands are not readily available like internal commands, but must be loaded just like any other program when you wish to use them.

If you have a diskette based system, i.e. no hard disk, you will need to insert your DOS diskette in drive A before issuing an external DOS command. If you have a hard disk, you will not need to take any special measures.

### DIR

DIR is the command used to display the contents of a disk.

### FORMAT

FORMAT is the command used to prepare new diskettes for use. With two different diskette sizes and both sizes having two different capacities, FORMAT has become a more difficult command to manage. How do you format a normal double density diskette in a high density diskette drive? All is explained more fully later on in the book.

## COPY

COPY is a very important command use to copy files to and from diskettes and hard disks.

## DEL

DEL is used to erase files from a hard disk or diskette.

## Filenames

Each file, which is a collection of data - e.g. a text - must have its own name. The rules for giving a file a name are that there can be up to 8 characters. The filename can then be extended (called the extension) with a full stop and 1, 2 or 3 more characters.

Avoid using unusual characters, use A-Z and 0-9 only. Use names that have some relation on the contents of the file, using X, X1, Y, etc., will make life difficult at a later stage. Two files can have the same filename if they are kept in different directories or on different diskettes, but this is an unwise policy as DOS cannot cope with two files with the same name in the same place.

## Wild cards *?

Wild cards are a means of imposing DOS commands on a group of files rather than on single files.

A question mark (?) is used to mean that any character in that position of the filename is acceptable, e.g.

| EXAMPLE?.DOC | matches |
|---|---|
| | EXAMPLE1.DOC |
| | EXAMPLE2.DOC |
| | EXAMPLEA.DOC |

An asterisk (*) is used to mean that any character combination in the rest of the file name or extension will do, e.g.

| EX*.D* | matches |
|---|---|
| | EXAMPLE1.DOC |
| | EXEGGS.DXX |
| | EXONE.DOC |

## Application programs

There are literally thousands of programs on the market today, but they mostly fall into a few main categories. In this section the main categories are summarised. Desktop publishing, communications and networks are discused more thoroughly.

| Program | Main uses |
|---|---|
| Word processing | creating texts |
| Spreadsheets | performing calculations and developing statistical models |
| Databases | storing and retrieving information |
| Desktop publishing | creating brochures, camera-ready copies, etc., combining both text and graphics |
| CAD | generating complex engineering drawings |
| Communications | allowing your computer to communicate with other ones |
| Graphics | creating statistical displays |
| Accounting | doing invoicing, balancing the books, etc. |

| Utility programs | designed to help you get the most out of your computer - copy files, make back-ups, menu programs to help you around your hard disk, personal organisers with diaries, telephone books and calculators - the list is almost endless. |
| --- | --- |
| Memory resident programs | programs that reside in the computer's memory - you load them once and then they are always available, even when you are running other application programs. |

# Desktop publishing

Desk top publishing is the art of producing printed matter - documents, books, brochures, etc., on a computer. Texts and pictures can be combined to complete a final original that can be printed directly from the computer, and/or sent off to a printers.

It is a fast growing area of computing, and programs and hardware exist to meet all levels of quality.

### Requirements

Firstly, desktop publishing requires a good fast AT or 286 computer at the very least. 386 machines are preferable for all but amateur productions.

Secondly, you will need a good desk top publishing program. Ventura Publisher from Rank Xerox, or Pagemaker from Aldus are the top professional software packages, but many smaller and cheaper programs exist and will suffice for lesser needs.

In desk top publishing texts and graphics are normally produced in separate programs, using the desk top publishing program to put the pieces together in a suitable layout. You will need a word processor to write your texts, and the desk top publishing program must be able to import (or use) files from your word processor. All desk top programmes can import ASCII files, and virtually all word processors can produce ASCII files, so you should be able to cope with smaller less well-known word processors and desk top publishing software

The same applies for graphics - you should produce graphs, diagrams and pictures with specialised graphics software, or scan in and edit pictures. These can then be imported into the desk top publishing software. However, there are numerous standards as far as graphics files are concerned, so it is well worth checking the standards to make sure potential programs are compatible.

A very important decision is the printer. Matrix printers are acceptable only for the most amateur publications, printouts take a long time and the quality is poor. Laser printers are, therefore, a must. There are two main sorts of laser printers, HP Laser Jet compatibles and Postscript printers. While Postscript printers are as much as twice as expensive, they do have several scaleable fonts (text types), 1-72 points for the knowledgeable, while HP Laser Jet compatibles are limited to a few fonts with sizes up to 24 pts (the same size as the main chapter headings in this book). HP Laser Jet compatibles can be extended with plug in cartridges. Both types can handle graphics competently.

Ordinary laser printers, with a resolution of 300 dpi (300 dots per inch) do not match up to the quality of a traditionally typeset work. Many printers can, however, handle diskettes containing desk top publishing files. So if you want a top quality production you can do all the work on your computer and hand over a diskette for the final production. Another possibility comes with the recent arrival of high resolution laser printers of up to 1000 dpi, which is marginally under the resolution of traditional typesetting. Of course these printers are expensive, but it is all a matter of what quality you wish the final product to have. Many computer books and other handbooks are produced with a standard 300 dpi laser printer.

An important extra for anyone dealing with graphics is a scanner.

# Communications

The whole idea of communications is to transfer data between two computers. For groups of computers within the same company, for example, this need is catered for by setting up networks (see next section). However, communications allows you to connect computers at any distance, even on the other side of the world.

The main reasons for computer communications are:

- Information retrieval, i.e. fetching information from any of the large information databases around the world.
- File transference, i.e. sending and receiving files of any type - documents, letters, accounts, drawings.
- Electronic mail, i.e. special systems for sending mail to other computer users.

## Requirements

As opposed to desk top publishing, communications is an inexpensive area of computing. Virtually any old computer will do, as long as it has a serial port or connector, as almost all computers have. Furthermore you need a modem and an ordinary telephone line.

A telephone line is suited to voices (analogue transmission, i.e. the sound can be varied without restriction), but a computer sends out digital impulses (i.e. the sound is restricted to minutely graded steps). That is where a modem comes in, to convert between digital and analogue sounds, enabling computers to send messages to each other.

Finally some communications software is needed. Often different programs for general communications, electronic mail and Videotext services may be required.

### Protocol

For communications to work, the computers in contact with each other must follow certain rules, called a protocol. These rules govern:

- Data transfer speed, i.e. the rate at which data is sent between the computers.
- The number of data bits and stop bits. Each unit of information sent contains a number of bits of information. The first bit is called a start bit, to warn the receiving computer that data is on its way. Next comes a string of actual data bit, 7 or 8 bits, which carry the information. After that there is one or two stop bits to tell the receiving computer that is the end of the information unit.
- The type of parity check. To check if data has been sent error free or not an elementary checking system is carried out. The parity bit is used to even out the number of zeros sent, or to make that number odd. Parity can thus be even, odd or none, i.e. no parity check is made.

## Networks

Networks differ from general communications by connecting two or more computers, often tens or even a hundred, so that they can share common information and accessories. Thus, for example, somebody working on station X can save a text file on a central file server, and that same file can be picked up and edited by a user on station F.

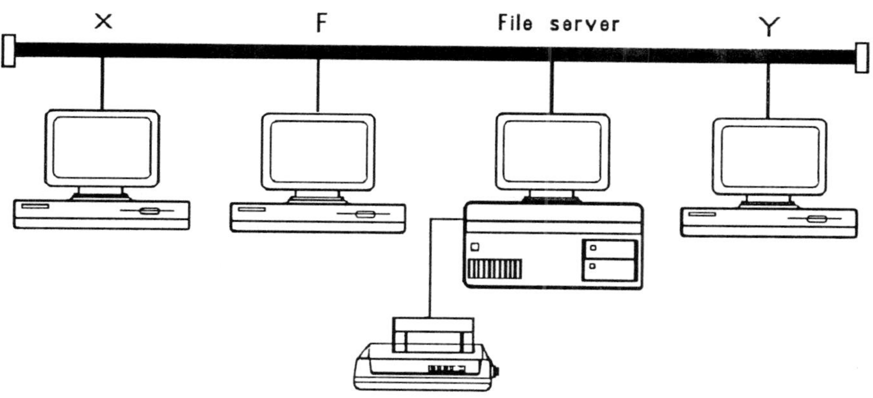

Networks normally also have a mailing system for sending mail to all users connected to the network.

Generally networks tend to cause a lot of problems, and having an appointed network supervisor is a must. However, the problems caused appear to be outweighed by the advantages or else networks would have died out long ago.

### Requirements

Networks require special add-in cards for each computer that is to be connected to the network. A difficult and often expensive part of building a network is the cable, as one cable that runs by all computers is necessary. Setting up a network in a large office can be tricky.

Furthermore a network program is needed, and needs to be set up for each computer.

For the simplest of needs, small network systems (e.g. just 2 computers) using the computers' serial ports can be set up extremely cheaply.

Finally, a lot of the software you use will require special network versions and licences.

## Programming

Programming is becoming more and more a job for professionals. Programs are becoming larger and more complicated in an attempt to use the computer to the best of its abilities. It would be very hard for a beginner to start creating his/her own programs and sell them. However, it is possible to write small individually adapted programs, although a lot of knowledge is required to write programs that do anything more than menial tasks.

### Programming languages

A programming language is a defined set of rules and instructions that can be used to write a program. Languages can be very different from one another, yet can accomplish the same goals.

The most common languages are:

- C
  Pascal
  Basic
  Prolog

You buy a programming language in the same way as you buy any other program.

### CASE tools

CASE stands for Computer Aided Software Engineering, which means that the computer actually assists you in devising and writing programs. In some cases you only need to choose via endless menus just what you want to do, and the CASE program creates the necessary computer program for you.

One example is Matrix Layout, an inexpensive CASE tool. Matrix makes you create programs by developing flow charts, choosing each step from a menu. It is possible to create perfectly adequate programs, including graphics, very easily, although some basic programming knowledge undoubtedly helps. Knowledge Pro from Knowledge Garden and Object Vision from Borland are other examples of such tools.

Such programming tools allow you reasonably easily to create simple, but professional looking programs that you can distribute to friends and colleagues, or even attempt to sell.

## Other terms

### AI and Expert systems

AI stands for Artificial Intelligence and is a science of its own that involves trying to make a computer think like a human being.

Expert systems is one type of program that comes under the wings of AI. The idea is that the knowledge of an expert, a person who is an expert in his own field, is programmed into a database of information. That information is then made available to other non-experts, who can draw on the knowledge for advice.

An expert system is not normally devised to replace a human, but to support one. Some examples would be:

An advisory system for doctors who through the years builds up a database of X-ray pictures. Perhaps five years later the same doctor has a doubt about a diagnosis and so searches the database for a similar picture to see how he diagnosed it before, and what happened afterwards. The same system could then be utilised by other doctors still learning the trade, as a teaching method or an advisory process.

On an oil rig, hundreds of readings and measurements must be continuously monitored. A human can easily cope with a dangerous reading, or even two, but what happens if six or seven emergencies arise at the same time? An expert system could give vital assistance by assessing the situation and giving clear instructions as to which faults should be dealt with first.

These are cases of very large and elaborate expert systems. However, many small expert systems are being developed, and companies in general are building more and more expert systems to cope with economic advice, fault finding and training systems to name but a few examples.

It is possible to buy ready made expert systems or even empty so-called expert system shells (from as little as £60) which you use to build your own applications.

## Benchmark

A benchmark is a test specifically designed to test the speed of a computer, or a particular function of a computer. Benchmarks give a way of comparing the speed of computers.

Two commonly accepted groups of tests which show the overall speed of a computer system are Landmark and the Norton SI index. They are often quoted in sales literature as an argument for buying a certain brand of computer and can generally be relied upon as a measure of the comparative speed of a computer.

## Buffer

A buffer is an intermediate storage area where data is temporarily stored. A printer buffer can store data that has been sent for printing.

A keyboard buffer stores key strokes when you type ahead of the program you are using. A screen buffer within a communications program will store a copy of one or more screen displays for later inspection.

DOS also uses buffers for storing data temporarily. Some larger programs require that you put a command in a special file called CONFIG.SYS to set up a minimum number of buffers that DOS uses. Some of these programs will edit or create the CONFIG.SYS file for you, for others you will have to do it yourself.

## Cache

Cache is a special sort of buffer used to speed up your computer. A computer often needs to read information stored on a hard disk or diskette and it has been found that as much as 80% of the time the very same information has been read before. Thus by setting up a buffer, each time the computer reads information the data is stored in the buffer. The next time the computer is to read information, it looks first in the buffer, or cache memory, to see if it is already stored there, which it often is. The data can be read from the cache memory, a much faster process than reading from a disk.

A special program is used to set aside a portion of the RAM memory as a cache memory. The larger the cache memory, the more chance there is of finding the data there and the faster the computer will be able to proceed. However, taking too large a cache memory will limit the amount of memory over to run programs, so a proper balance is needed for each individual system. As a rule 64 kb is a good size.

The 80486 processor has a cache memory built into it adding to the overall speed of such a system.

## Co-processor

A co-processor, as its name suggests, is a help processor to the main processor. In normal terms this usually means a mathematical co-processor that does calculations more quickly and accurately than the standard processor, and releases the standard processor to perform other instructions.

Mathematical co-processors speed the computer up if used with large spreadsheets and CAD/CAM programs. However, the applications program must be specially programmed to use the co-processor, it is not something that happens automatically.

Most computers have an empty socket on the motherboard, the main circuit board inside the CPU, into which the co-processor very simply pushed into. When buying a co-processor you should make sure that its speed corresponds to the speed of the main processor.

The 80486 processor has a mathematical co-processor built in to it.

## EISA and MCA

From the beginning of the PC world, computers have been developed along the lines of existing models. Recently, however, IBM developed a new internal structure, MCA or Micro Channel Architecture, to improve the overall performance of PCs. Unfortunately this change meant that many computer accessories (add-in cards) used in standard computers could not be transferred or used in the new MCA computers.

A group of other large computer manufacturing companies got together and decided to develop their own computer architecture EISA in competition with IBM's MCA. EISA has the advantage of being compatible with the current computer architecture found in virtually all computers.

For the user, this means that if he/she buys a new computer in the future that has an EISA architecture, all the accessories from the old computer can be moved into the new EISA computer.

## EPROM

Earlier in this chapter we explained ROM, Read Only Memory. These are chips that are manufactured with a program in them. A PROM is a Programmable ROM. This means that it is empty when it has been manufactured, but can be programmed with the help of a special unit called an EPROM programmer. When the PROM has been programmed, then it is programmed for always, just like a ROM.

An EPROM takes this idea one step further and is an Erasable Programmable ROM. That is, it can be programmed like a PROM, but also the program can be removed and the EPROM re-programmed. Erasure is done by a short exposure (5-15 mins.) to ultra-violet light.

## Interactive video

Interactive video is a combination of a computer and a video working together. A typical system will be a some sort of training system, where your reactions to a certain situation govern how the next situation is presented.

The computer assesses the answers supplied and moves the video to the right position to show the next sequence of pictures.

## Multi-media system

Multi-media systems look set to become the product of the nineties. Basically this means that you can connect tv, video, video cameras and music synthesizers to your computer.

It will be possible to "grab" pictures from a tv, video or camera, to edit the pictures in your computer and create animated or moving picture sequences, add text, save it all on video, add some sounds and show it all on tv.

All of these individual processes can be done today, and complete multi-media systems are available for £2000 or more. The next few years will, however, see strong development in the area.

## NLQ

NLQ stands for Near Letter Quality and is a term used to describe one of the features of a matrix printer. By printing a line twice but offsetting the second print slightly, a printout of much higher quality is produced.

## Non-interruptable power supply

A real problem for computer users is the power supply. Surges, falls and power cuts can cause the computer to go down (turn off) or to lose or damage data. Many companies now protect themselves against this by buying non-interruptable power supply units that monitor the current and level it off. Furthermore within microseconds of a complete power failure, batteries are switched in to keep the computer system going for fifteen to twenty minutes, giving everyone time to save the work they are currently doing and stop using the computer.

## Postscript

Postscript is a special programming language for producing printouts on laser printers. It is a page description language, which means that a whole page is formed before being printed, as opposed to a matrix printer printing one line at a time.

A Postscript laser printer is a very common printer for those producing documents, books, brochures, etc. Character fonts can be scaled up and down to print very large or very small letters, and pictures are printed with a high quality.

Postscript lasers are expensive, £3000 or more, but for the professional provide a high quality printout.

## RISC

RISC stands for Reduced Instruction Set Computer. As processors have been developed they have been given more and more basic instructions that they can perform. Processors became more and more complex. RISC meant that the processor was given instead very few basic instructions which could be performed at far higher speeds. The computer became faster but more difficult to develop programs for.

## Unix

Unix is an alternative operating system to DOS. Originally for mini-computers, it is now available on PCs.

## Waitstates

You may well have heard the term waitstates and wondered what it really is. The computer's memory chips have their own specification and limits as to what speed they can reliably work at. Typical values are 80 ns (nanoseconds), 100ns, 120ns and higher. The numbers refer to the amount of time it takes to access data from a memory chip. The higher the value the slower the data access.

Processors have been getting faster and faster, and so the rate at which they need to fetch data form the memory chips has also increased. At some point, depending on the combination of the speed of the processor and the access speed of the memory chips, the processor is actually trying to get data faster than it can be accessed. This state of affairs means that data access becomes unreliable.

To avoid this situation a waitstate is introduced, that it the processor is given an idle task to do in order to slow down its request for data, and the memory chips can cope. This means that the whole computer system works more slowly.

Thus, 0 Waitstates has become an important selling point in advertisements. A computer working with 0 waitstates is not slowed down when fetching data from memory chips. A 12 MHz computer with 1 waitstate may well be a slower computer than a 10 MHz system with 0 waitstates.

Why do waitstates exist? Because by introducing 1 waitstate the manufacturer can use much cheaper and slower memory chips, and thus produce a cheaper computer.

# 2. Batch Files and AUTOEXEC.BAT

You may well have heard the term *batch file* and wondered what it really meant, or even have some understanding but assumed it was too difficult to get involved in. In this chapter the simplicity and usefulness of batch files is revealed. You can learn how quickly you can create batch files and by studying a few examples you will soon be able to write your own.

The all-important batch file called AUTOEXEC.BAT is also covered.

Finally, the last section of this chapter delves deeper into the world of batch files and presents the batch file commands that are available if you wish to start creating small batch file programs.

## What is a batch file

A batch file is a sort of auto-pilot that can perform several DOS commands in sequence. If you are regularly typing in a series of DOS commands, for example to change directories and start a certain program, then you should think about creating a batch file to do the repetitive work for you. Then, instead of typing in the commands, you only need to type the name of your batch file and the rest is done for you.

Here is a quick example: Assume that you have a computer game on your hard disk called CHASE.EXE, and that it is stored in a subdirectory called \GAMES\CHASE. To start the game, you would normally have to go through the following steps:

- Type `c:` to make C the current drive.
- Press the ↵ key.
- Type `cd \games\chase` to move to the CHASE subdirectory.

- Press the ↵ key.
- Type `chase` to start the game.
- Press the ↵ key.

This is not really hard work, but nevertheless can cause a few problems for a user not really conversant with DOS commands. The whole process could be replaced by one batch file named CHASE.BAT. The batch file would have the following contents:

```
c:
cd \games\chase
chase
cd\
```

Comparing the batch file to the commands above you will see that exactly the same three commands are used. A fourth command, **cd**, is added to the end - this changes the current directory back to the root directory at when you exit the CHASE program. So batch files can follow commands to start a program and even resume control when that program is ended.

The greatest difference is that when you wished to start the game you would only have to type one command, chase, and then press the ↵ key.

Using batch files to start programs that otherwise involve giving three or four DOS commands is one obvious use. More examples will be given later on in this chapter, and examples of batch files will also appear in other chapters.

## How to create batch files

There are three different ways of creating a batch file, they are:

- Using your word processor.
- Using the DOS command COPY.
- Using the DOS program EDLIN.

Two of these methods are explained briefly below.

## Using your word processor

Using your word processor has the advantage that you already know how to use it. It is easy to create both small and large batch files especially if your batch file contains information to be displayed on the screen and you wish to give it some sort of layout.

However, there is one restriction on using your word processor - the file you produce has to be an ASCII file. An ASCII file is quite simply a clean text file free from any special control characters. Most word processors add their own such control characters to texts and hide them automatically from you. However, most word processors also have the ability to produce ASCII code. You may need to check your word processor manual to find out about this.

You can also use an Editor program, which is a kind of word processor anyway. Editors always produce clean ASCII files.

To produce a batch file with your word processor/editor do as follows:

- Start your word processor and open a new file.
- Type in the commands.
- Save the file as an ASCII file giving it a suitable name with a .BAT extension, e.g. CHASE.BAT.

Note that the batch file should be saved in the root directory of your hard disk, or if you have one, in a special subdirectory called \BATCH where you gather all your batch files.

If you have a diskette based system you should put the batch file on the diskette containing the relevant program.

## Using the COPY command

Normally you use the COPY command to copy files to and from diskettes and hard disks. By using the COPY command together with the word CON (short for console, i.e. your keyboard), you still copy a file, but that file comes directly from the keyboard as you type it in.

It is very quick and easy to create a file using COPY. COPY is an internal DOS command, which means that it is always readily available even if you are using a diskette based system. It is ideal for creating small batch files containing just a few lines, or larger ones if you type carefully and accurately. The reason is that the COPY command allows you to enter text one line at a time and having confirmed that line by pressing the ↵ key, you cannot go back to it to change it in any way. If you make a mistake the only thing to do is to end the file and start all over again.

As an example of how to create a file in this way, do as follows:

- Type:

  `copy con example.txt`

- Press the ↵ key.

This has opened a file called EXAMPLE.TXT, i.e. not a batch file in this case. The cursor has moved down to the next blank line is waiting for you to type in the first line.

```
C:\copy con example.txt
_
```

- Type:

  `I am creating this file using the COPY command`

At this point, i.e. before you confirm the line by pressing the ↵ key, you can still edit the line by deleting with the backspace (⇐) key.

- Use the backspace (⇐) key to remove command, but not the space after COPY.

- Now type:

  `CON command.`

- Press the ↵ key.

The first line is now confirmed and cannot be edited.

- Type:

  `This is the second line`

- Press the ↵ key.

- Type:

  `Bye for now`

- Press the ↵ key.

That is enough for this file. To end the file do as follows:

- Press the **F6** key.

Pressing the **F6** key tells DOS that you do not wish to enter any more lines. **F6** is represented on the screen by ^z. The result of your work should look like this:

```
C:\copy con example.txt
I am creating this file using the COPY command
This is the second line
Bye for now
^Z
```

- Finally, press the ↵ key to end the whole command.

You have now created a text file. To assure yourself of the file's existence, do as follows:

- Type:

  `type example.txt`

- Press the ↵ key.

The file will be displayed on your screen.

If you wish to delete the file, do as follows:

- Type:

  `del example.txt`

- Press the ↵ key.

The file will be deleted from your diskette or hard disk.

## Using EDLIN

EDLIN is a line processor supplied with DOS. It lies between a word processor and using the COPY CON command. You can enter commands line by line, as with COPY CON, but each line can be edited just as with a word processor. However, it is not as simple as moving the cursor up and down. A command has to be given to move to any specific line, and you will inevitably need to learn a small set of commands to work with EDLIN.

EDLIN is not covered in this book but will appear in a more specialised book on DOS in this series of books. If you wish to find out more about EDLIN now, you should consult your DOS manual.

## How batch files work

A batch file is a special file containing a series of commands. All batch files must have a filename with a .BAT extension, i.e. CHASE.BAT, WORD.BAT, FMT.BAT, etc.

When you wish to run a batch file you simply type the name of that batch file - just the main filename is necessary, you do not need to type the .BAT extension part of the filename. For example, type chase, word, fmt, etc.

When DOS finds the batch file (assuming you have the right diskette loaded or have not hidden the batch file in a subdirectory somewhere on your hard disk), it reads the commands one line at a time and tries to execute that command. If, for any reason, DOS cannot follow the command, it will issue a message and move on to the next command on the next line.

If during the batch file process you remove the diskette containing the batch file, you may for example use the batch file to start another program that requires access to other diskettes, then you will need to re-insert the batch file diskette before DOS continues with the next command.

- Batch files can be aborted by pressing **Ctrl + C**.

## Some example batch files

Try creating some of the following example batch files using the COPY CON command. The first two examples contain step-by-step instructions, the following examples list only the contents of each file.

### Example 1

Assume that you have a hard disk and a word processor called WORDPROC in a subdirectory named \WORDP. The following batch file will help you to start your word processing file with one simple command. Obviously, if you want to adapt the file to your own computer set up, you will have to replace the subdirectory and program names, and even the drive designation (if, for example, your word processor is stored on drive D). You can also give the batch file a different name if you wish. Do as follows:

- Type:

  `c:`

- Press the ↵ key.
- Type:

  `cd \`

- Press the ↵ key.

These two first steps merely make sure that C is the current drive and that the root directory \ is the current directory, so that the batch file is created and stored in the root directory. This should not be confused with the first commands in the actual batch file.

- Type:

  `copy con wordp.bat`

- Press the ↵ key.
- Type:

  `c:`

- Press the ↵ key.
- Type:

  `cd \wordp`

- Press the ↵ key.
- Type:

  `wordproc`

- Press the ↵ key.
- Type:

  `cd\`

- Press the ↵ key.
- Press the **F6** key.
- Press the ↵ key.

The batch file is now complete. To run the batch file simply type `wordp` or any other name you have given the file.

### Example 2

Example 2 assumes the following: You have a computer with two 5.25" diskette drives, and a word processor program called WORDPROC on a diskette. The word processor requires the program diskette in drive A, and a document diskette in drive B. You wish to create a batch file on your word processor diskette that first checks to see if there is a document diskette in drive B with suitable free space available. You will do this by pausing to ask the user to insert a diskette in drive B, then giving the DIR command to list the files on B and show the available storage space.

- Insert your system diskette in drive A.
- Type:

  ```
  a:
  ```

- Press the ↵ key.

The first step merely ensures that A is the current drive so that the batch file is created and stored on the diskette in drive A. This should not be confused with the first command in the actual batch file.

- Type:

  ```
  copy con wordp.bat
  ```

- Press the ↵ key.
- Type:

  ```
  a:
  ```

- Press the ↵ key.

You will now introduce the PAUSE command, which means that DOS will stop and wait for a key to be pressed. This gives you the opportunity to display a message. The text "Strike any key to continue" is added automatically by DOS on the next line immediately after your message.

- Type:

  ```
  pause  Insert document diskette in drive B
  ```

- Press the ↵ key.
- Type:

  ```
  dir b:
  ```

- Press the ↵ key.

The pause command is important again to give the user a chance to see the result of the DIR command - otherwise DOS would just go ahead with the next batch file command.

- Type:

  ```
  pause  Check free space, Cancel with Ctrl-C, or
  ```

- Press the ↵ key.
- Type:

  ```
  wordproc
  ```

- Press the ↵ key.
- Press the **F6** key.
- Press the ↵ key.

The batch file is now complete. To run the batch file simply type `wordp` or any other name you have given the file.

## Example 3

This next example assumes that you are working with a project on your word processor which involves several document files. At the end of each day, you wish to make a back-up copy of these document files. A batch file will help you with this process.

The following assumptions are made: You have a hard disk (a similar example with diskettes only follows) and a word processor program called WORDPROC. Your project files all have filenames starting PROJ and extensions .DOC (e.g. PROJ01.DOC, PROJ02.DOC, etc.).

The project files are stored along with the word processor program in the \WORDPR subdirectory. Here is a complete listing of the creation of the relevant batch file, which should be created in the root directory or \BATCH subdirectory if you have one:

```
c:\copy con prjcopy.bat
pause  Place back-up diskette in drive A.
copy c:\wordpr\proj*.doc a:/v
^Z
```

If you have a diskette based computer you could do the same thing, but copy the files from drive B to drive A. One reason for doing it this way is that it is likely that after finishing work with your word processor your document diskette will already be in drive B. Create the batch file on the document diskette in drive B, and run it from drive b, i.e. type b: before creating or running the batch file.

```
B:copy con prjcopy.bat
pause  Place back-up diskette in drive A.
copy b:proj*.doc a:/v
^Z
```

# AUTOEXEC.BAT

There is one particular batch file that you will almost certainly have heard of - AUTOEXEC.BAT. This batch file is very special because DOS always looks for it when you start your computer, and then follows the instructions given in it. Thus AUTOEXEC.BAT can be used to automatically run a program, or perform other commands, each time you start your computer.

**If you have a hard disk**, you will find AUTOEXEC.BAT in the root directory. Do as follows to list it:

- Type:

  `cd\`

- Press the ↵ key.
- Type:

  `type autoexec.bat`

- Press the ↵ key.

**If you have a diskette based system**, you will find AUTOEXEC.BAT on your system diskette, if it exists. Do as follows to list it:

- Insert your system diskette in drive A.
- Type:

  `a:`
- Press the ↵ key.
- Type:

  `type autoexec.bat`
- Press the ↵ key.

**In both cases**, if the AUTOEXEC.BAT file exists (it will almost certainly do so), then its contents will be listed. It is impossible to say what the file will contain on any individual computer as it is possible to set up this file to suit your personal needs. Here is an example of a typical AUTOEXEC.BAT file:

```
ECHO OFF
CLS
PROMPT $P$G
PATH C:\;C:\BATCH;C:\DOS;\UTILITY;\pctools;
mode com1:96,n,8,1
KEYBUK
\mouse\mouse.com
MENU
```

`ECHO OFF` The meaning of this command is covered in the next section, it tells DOS not to display (ECHO) each command on the screen.

`CLS` Clears the screen

`PROMPT $P$G` Produces the extended system prompt to include the current subdirectory (a must for hard disk users).

`PATH C:\;C:\BATCH;C:\DOS;\UTILITY;\pctools;`

The PATH command can be followed by a list of drives and directories that DOS is to search through to try to find a program. This example includes the root directory (C:\), a subdirectory obviously formed to hold batch files (C:\BATCH), and the DOS directory (C:\DOS). This means that when a command to start a program or a batch file is given, if DOS cannot immediately find the file it will start searching other subdirectories in the order given in this list. See also the section **The PATH command** later on in this chapter.

`mode com1:96,n,8,1`
Here the DOS command MODE is used to set up serial port No. 1, probably for communications purposes, or even to be connected to a serial printer.

`KEYBUK` A command like this will be found on all computers not using U.S. keyboards. KEYBUK, or a similar command is used to load a program that re-maps the keyboard to a specific national layout.

`\mouse\mouse.com`
This command loads a mouse driver program found in the \MOUSE subdirectory.

`MENU` Finally the command MENU indicates that the user wishes a menu program to be started.

This list is just one example of how useful batch files can be - imagine having to type in that lot each time you start your computer!

AUTOEXEC.BAT can be created and edited in your word processor (ASCII mode) or using COPY CON or EDLIN. Some programs will even automatically add lines to it when you install them.

If you wish to experiment with your AUTOEXEC.BAT file make a copy of it on a diskette somewhere first, than if you really mess things up you can always restore the original. You can quickly make a copy as follows (assuming that AUTOEXEC.BAT is on the current drive/directory):

- Type:

  ```
  copy autoexec.bat ae.bat
  ```

- Press the ↵ key.

If needed you can reinstall your original AUTOEXEC.BAT file with the following command:

- Type:

  ```
  copy ae.bat autoexec.bat
  ```

- Press the ↵ key.

## Batch file commands

There are several commands that you can use in batch files apart from starting programs, changing drives and directories and using other common DOS commands. These are covered briefly in this section. The commands are:

- CALL
  ECHO
  FOR
  GOTO
  IF
  PAUSE
  REM
  SHIFT

The commands are not explained in depth in this book but will appear in a more specialised book on DOS in this series of books. If you wish to find out more about them now, you should consult your DOS manual which has a chapter specific to batch processing.

### CALL

The CALL command is used from within one batch file to run another. When completed, control will return to the initial batch file.

Example:

```
cls
call fmt
cls
call prjcopy
```

### ECHO

Normally, commands in a batch file are displayed (echoed) on the screen. To tidy up a screen display you can use the ECHO OFF to stop the commands being displayed. Then you can use the ECHO command together with a message to display that message on the screen. Finally by giving the ECHO ON command, the echo function is restored and commands will once again be displayed on your screen.

Example:

```
echo off
echo * Project Copier *
echo ==================
echo *                *
prjcopy
```

## REM

REM can be used to display a message, rather like ECHO. If ECHO is OFF, then REM lines will not be displayed. REM without a following message will produce a blank line on the screen.

Example:

```
rem
rem  Project Copier
rem  ==============
rem
prjcopy
```

## PAUSE

PAUSE, as you have already seen, suspends execution of the batch file until the user presses a key. A message can also follow the PAUSE command and that message will be displayed on the screen together with a "Strike any key to continue..." message on the next line.

Example:

```
echo off
echo * Project Copier *
echo ==================
echo *                *
pause * Insert backup diskette in drive A *
prjcopy
```

## GOTO

A batch file can be divided into two or more units, each unit has a special label that identifies it. A colon (:) at the start of a line denotes the start of such a unit, and the label, or unit name, follows the colon.

GOTO allows you to move to any label within the batch file.

Example:

```
echo off
:dirloop
cls
echo * Insert diskette in drive A *
pause
dir a:/p
goto dirloop
```

This little program is a loop that never ends. Every time execution gets to the last line it is redirected to the dirloop label (:dirloop) and everything starts again. It could be used to continually check the contents of diskettes. To exit this batch file, you would have to press **Ctrl + C**.

## IF

IF performs a command based on the result of a condition. IF NOT performs the command when the condition is false. The condition may be an errorlevel, not discussed here, a test to see if a file exists, or two variables being equal.

Example: IF EXIST / IF NOT EXIST

This batch file makes a back up copy of the file PRICES.DAT, if it exists, or displays a message if not.

```
if exist prices.dat goto cop
if not exist prices.dat goto nocop
:cop
pause * Insert backup diskette in drive A *
copy prices.dat a:/v
goto end
:nocop
echo Can't find data file PRICES.DAT
:end
```

Notice the **:end** label is empty, i.e. no commands follow. It is there so that after a successful copy execution can be passed over the **:nocop** label to the end label, where the batch file, with no more commands to perform, ends.

Example: Variables

When starting a batch file you normally just type the name of that file, without its extension. However, batch files are capable of reading variables, or parameters, that follow the batch filename. For example, you may wish to make a back up copy of your project files onto a diskette, but sometimes copy only the .DOC files and sometimes all the files. This could be handled by typing in a parameter for your batch file to assess.

Imagine that the batch file is called PRJBACK.BAT. To make a full copy you type prjback all, to copy only the document files you type prjback docs, and leave the batch file to sort out the rest.

The parameters are numbered %1 to %9 as they appear on the command line, %0 is reserved for the batch filename. Thus typing prjback all will mean that %1 is assigned the value "all", and this can be tested for in an IF command.

This is what the file could look like:

```
echo off
cls
echo Insert backup diskette in drive A
pause
if "%1" == "all" goto :all
if "%1" == "docs" goto :docs
goto missing

:all
copy *.* a:/v
goto end

:docs
copy *.doc a:/v
goto end

:missing
echo Parameter wrong or missing
echo Type prjback all, or prjback docs

:end
echo Finished.
```

If the parameter "all" is found then execution is passed (goto) to the **:all** label.

If the parameter "docs" is found then execution is passed (goto) to the **:docs** label.

If neither parameter is found then execution is passed to the :missing label, and a message is displayed.

### SHIFT

Shift is used to break the limit of 10 parameters, by shifting them one place. Thus parameters that appear after the tenth (%9) will be shifted one at a time into %9.

### FOR

FOR is one of the more advanced commands used for performing operations on groups of files. It is not explained more here.

## Placing and running batch files

When creating a batch file you must decide where to put it, i.e. in which subdirectory or on which diskette.

For diskette based systems it is usually most useful to save the batch file on the diskette containing the program(s) to which it relates. When running the batch file it is simply a matter of inserting the correct diskette and starting the batch file by typing its name.

For hard disk systems there is more choice. You could save the batch file in the subdirectory related to the program(s). This would mean that you would still have to change subdirectories before running it unless you use the PATH command to help the computer find the batch file - see next section.

A second and more normal approach is to save all batch files in the root directory and use the batch file itself to change subdirectories as necessary. This will also require the help of the PATH command if your batch files do not automatically change to the root directory on completion.

Another common choice is to create a special subdirectory called \BATCH and save all batch files there. The batch files will need to contain all the necessary commands for changing subdirectories as necessary. The PATH command will also be needed.

# The PATH command

The PATH command is an internal DOS command. It is used to help the computer find programs and batch files. When instructed to start a batch file or a program, DOS will always look in the current drive and subdirectory to find the required file. If it is not there then the message `File not found` will be issued. PATH allows you to give a list of drives and subdirectories to be searched after the current drive/subdirectory if the file is not found.

A typical PATH command would look like this:

```
PATH C:\;C:\DOS;C:\BATCH
```

Each named subdirectory is separated by a semi-colon ;. Thus if you gave the command GO the computer would search the disk for the file GO.BAT, GO.EXE or GO.COM in the following order:

```
the current subdirectory
the root directory (C:\)
the DOS directory (C:\DOS)
the BATCH directory (C:\BATCH)
```

It is possible to add as many subdirectories as you wish - indeed, some programs do this automatically for you when you install them.

The PATH command can be typed whenever the DOS prompt is displayed. However, it does replace any current PATH command which is active. It is normal to have this PATH command in the AUTOEXEC.BAT file so that it is automatically activated each time you start the computer.

# More example batch files

### Example 4a

This example will display only the executable programs (.EXE and .COM files) on the current drive/directory:

```
echo off
cls
echo directory of .EXE files
echo ----------------------
dir *.exe/p
pause press any key for .COM files
cls
echo directory of .COM files
echo ----------------------
dir *.com/p
```

### Example 4b

To improve the example 4a and allow the directory listings for a diskette in drive A or B you can allow the batch file to take a variable (%1) and act accordingly.

```
echo off
cls
echo directory of .EXE files on drive %1
echo ---------------------------------
dir %1:*.exe/p
pause press any key for .COM files
cls
echo directory of .COM files on drive %1
echo ---------------------------------
dir %1:*.com/p
```

Now by typing the batch filename (here assumed to be EC.BAT) and the drive letter the %1 is replaced by the drive. Thus

| | |
|---|---|
| `ec a` | gives the listing of drive A |
| `ec b` | gives the listing of drive B |
| `ec c` | gives the listing of drive C - current subdirectory |

It is very easy to write a similar batch file, for example, to display all .DOC or all .PCX files only.

### Example 5

To build a simple menu system you only need a few batch files. Basically the main batch file is used to display the actual menu. Then one small batch file for each menu entry is used to start the required program.

In this example it is assumed that you wish to have the following menu choices:

1. Word processor
2. Spreadsheet
3. Format diskette in drive A:
4. Total back-up

By then typing the relevant number the desired program should be started. Thus typing 1 (and ↵) will start a batch file called 1.BAT that starts the word processor. Typing 2 starts 2.BAT, etc.

All five batch files for such a system are given here, but remember they are only examples and must be adapted for your own use. It is even possible to build complicated systems, with many batch files, but if it gets too complicated then it would be better to invest in a menu type program (see chapter entitled **Hard Disks**).

Finally, to run the menu system you need to type MENU (i.e. the main batch file is called MENU.BAT) - which can even be placed in the AUTOEXEC.BAT file.

**The main batch file called MENU.BAT**

```
echo off
cls
c:
cd\
echo  MENU SYSTEM
echo  -----------
echo  1. Word processing
echo  2. Spreadsheet
echo  3. Format diskette in drive A:
echo  4. Total back-up
echo  -----------
echo  Type the desired number and then press ENTER
```

**The word processing batch file called 1.BAT**

```
cd\wordproc
wp
cd\
menu
```

**The spreadsheet batch file called 2.BAT**

```
cd\sprd
sp
cd\
menu
```

A system was jointly developed by three leading computer companies - Lotus, Intel and Microsoft, and was called the LIM (or LIM-EMS) specification. This allowed a further 15 Mb to be added to the then current limit of 1 Mb. However, DOS could not use this extra memory - it could only use the 64 kb block. Thus the 64 kb block was used to mirror any other 64 kb block of memory from the total of 15 Mb. This meant that large amount of memory could be stored in the 15 Mb memory area, and the 64 kb block was a sort of 'window', that could look at any 64 kb section of the 15 Mb memory and copy it to the 64 kb block that DOS could access. It was now possible to store large amounts of data, but no programs could be run in this new memory area, only data stored.

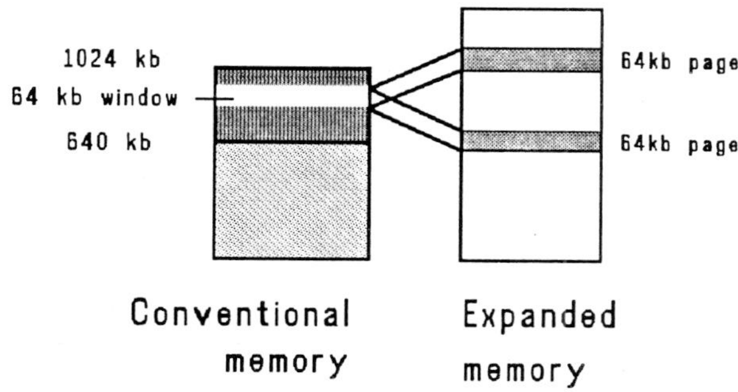


## Expanded memory

The 15 Mb extra memory available as described above is known as expanded memory, and is easy to confuse with extended memory, that is explained in the next section. Thus expanded memory provided for the memory increase by 'swapping' 64 kb blocks into the standard memory area that DOS can use. This is often referred to as *page framing*. Each 64 kb block of data is known as a page and the 64 kb block within the standard memory that DOS can use is the *page frame*.

For program developers expanded memory constituted a vast improvement on the previous limitations, but some developers found that the benefits were not as great as they wished. Only being able to mirror one 64 kb page at a time still hindered development. A new initiative was taken by three other companies - AST, Ashton Tate and Quadram, which allowed multiple 64 kb pages to be 'mapped' (or mirrored) at the same time. Even the first 640 kb of memory could be used as a page frame. This specification was named EEMS - Enhanced Expanded Memory Specification. Lotus, Intel and Microsoft responded by improving there LIM specification to encompass all the advantages of the EEMS specification.

With so much memory available and accessible *multitasking* came of age. Multitasking is the ability to run several programs at the same time, and swap between them at will. This will investigated further at the end of the chapter.

### Extended memory

Unfortunately for many computer users the two methods of increasing memory - expanded and extended memory - are so alike in name that it can be very confusing.

Extended memory came to life with the introduction of the 80286 processor (the first AT computers). This processor is actually capable of addressing 16 Mb of memory although DOS itself can only address the first 1 Mb. Confused? Read on. To cope with this the processor had two 'modes'. The *real mode* operates when you are running DOS with only the first 1 Mb accessible. The other 15 Mb are made accessible by operating the processor in the so-called *protected mode*. Thus extended memory is memory found over and above the 1 Mb barrier and is only accessible in the protected mode. Still confused?

## Memory organisation

At this point it is time for a brief summary of just how computer memory is organised.

The first 640 kb of memory is known as *conventional* memory. This is the area used to load and run your programs. Although most computers these days are supplied with a full 640 kb, it is possible to buy one with only 256 kb (rare) or 512 kb (more common) or even some other amount. So the conventional memory does not have to be fully filled, the less conventional memory your computer has the less room there is to run your programs.

The next area between 640 kb and up to 1024 kb (or 1 Mb) is reserved for the system to run video cards, hard disks and other basic processes (BIOS). As discussed earlier there are gaps of unused memory within this area.

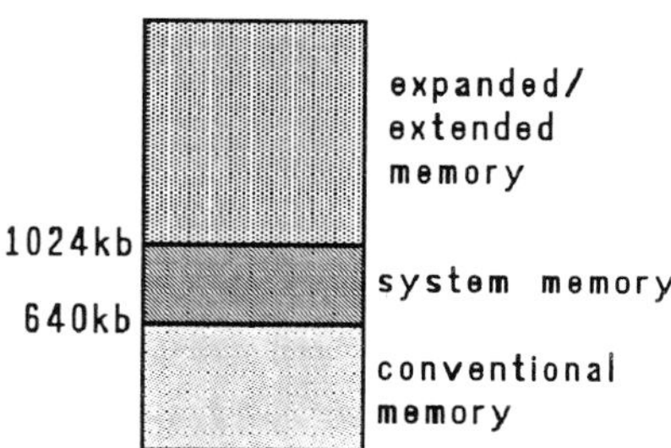


Extended memory can be installed directly above the 1 Mb area and up to the 16 Mb limit. Extended memory can only be accessed by processors that have a protected mode (80286 and later, e.g. 386 and 486 machines).

Expanded memory can also be installed above the 1 Mb area. Expanded memory is used to swap pages, or blocks of data, into the memory below 1 Mb so that DOS can readily use it.

## How DOS and memory resident programs affect the available memory

When thinking in terms of available memory it is important to fix your mind on conventional memory as this is where programs are loaded and run. Let's now assume that your computer has 640 kb conventional memory - if it hasn't then the following discussion still applies in full.

As soon as you start your computer DOS will load itself and take a sizeable chunk of your conventional memory in doing so. As a rule, the more recent the version of DOS, e.g. version 3.3 is more recent than version 2.1, the more memory DOS will steal. DOS could take as much as 90 kb.

Other small programs may also be loaded automatically when you start your computer. These can include device drivers, for example a mouse, a special screen driver or a keyboard program if you have a non-USA keyboard. All these small and necessary programs take conventional memory.

Memory resident programs, i.e. programs that reside in memory and are always available whatever program you are running, also take their share of conventional memory. A menu program may take 35 kb, a personal organiser with a diary, address book and calculator may require a further 50 kb. You may have a communications program running in the 'background' which could cost perhaps 45 kb. If you are connected to a network a further 60 kb or so will be needed. So you see each memory resident program steals conventional memory and the less conventional memory available the less room there is to run your programs.

For example, after loading DOS and a few other small programs you may have 460 kb conventional memory available. This is fine for most application programs, but you will not be able to run some of the largest and most professional programs, or some programs may be 'slowed down' as the lack of available memory means data must temporarily be stored on disk. If your computer has less than 640 kb conventional memory the total available memory will be lower and even more programs will be affected.

# 4. Diskettes and Drives

This chapter is dedicated to diskettes, diskette drives, formatting diskettes and the various associated problems.

## Diskettes

A diskette is a thin round plastic disc coated with a very thin film containing millions of magnetic particles. Data is stored on the diskette by magnetising these particles. The particles are arranged in a number of tracks, or concentric rings, on both sides of the diskette.

When you buy a new diskette it naturally has no data stored on it, just a number of empty concentric tracks. Furthermore, DOS requires the diskette to be divided into small areas (sectors) that are easy to work with. Thus a new diskette has to be prepared for use, this is called formatting. Even used diskettes with information stored on them can be formatted. This results in all stored data being wiped out as the diskette is re-formatted.

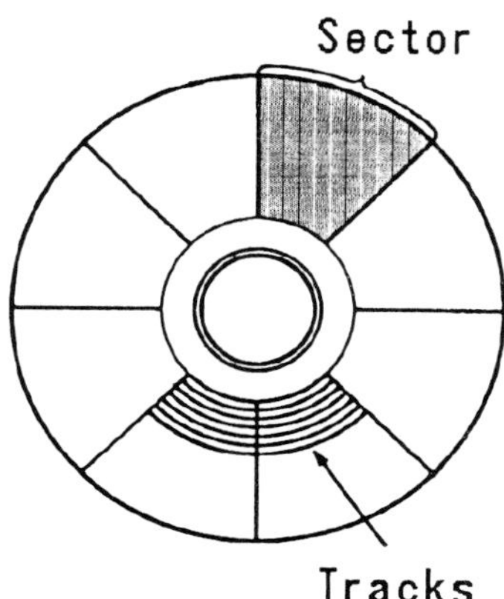


For a standard 5.25" diskette each track is divided up into 9 segments, or sectors, each storing 512 kb of data. Thus a standard 5.25" diskette with 40 tracks per side would be able to store 40 tracks x 9 sectors x 512 kb x 2 sides = 368 640 bytes.

There are two diskette sizes, the old standard 5.25" and the new standard 3.5". The 3.5" diskettes have taken over because of their smaller format, they can store more information than the 5.25" diskettes, and because the hard plastic casing offers far better protection than their floppy 5.25" counterparts.

# Disk organization

When you format a diskette, DOS divides that diskette into four different areas, the *boot record*, the *File Allocation Table* (FAT), the *root directory*, and the *data area*. Note that the following explanations also apply for a hard disk.

The outside track, nearest the outside edge, is known as track 0. The first sector of the first track is called sector 1.

## The boot record

The boot record occupies sector 1 of track 0 on a diskette. It contains a short program that in its turn reads the system files necessary to start the computer. It also contains some vital information about the diskette itself. This information is so important that it is written to all diskettes, even those that are not system diskettes.

## FAT (File Allocation Table)

The FAT maintains information on each sector of the diskette - whether it is data is stored in a particular sector or if the sector is free to be used. When formatting a diskette all sectors are tested by DOS and any faulty sectors are marked as 'bad' in the FAT thus making sure that the sector is not used to store information.

## The root directory

Formatting a diskette also creates a root directory. Here information is stored on each file found on the diskette - the filename and its extension, the date and time of its creation, the size of the file and where on the diskette the program starts.

The size of the root directory is fixed during formatting. For example, a 360 kb diskette will have room for 112 file entries, a 30 Mb hard disk room for 512 entries. If you create a subdirectory, then it is created in the data area on the diskette.

## The data area

The fourth and final area of a diskette is the data area, which takes up the rest of the diskette space. It is used to store data - programs and data files, and information on any subdirectories created.

## Diskette storage capacity

Both 5.25" and 3.5" diskettes have two different types of diskette which can store differing amounts of data.

There are standard diskettes (often called double density or DD) and high-density diskettes (HD). The following table shows how much each size and type of diskette can store.

| Size | Type | Storage capacity |
|---|---|---|
| 5.25" | standard (DD) | 360 kb |
| 5.25" | high-density (HD) | 1.2 Mb (1200 kb) |
| 3.5" | standard (DD) | 720 kb |
| 3.5" | high-density (HD) | 1.44 Mb (1440 kb) |

The higher capacities are enabled by cramming more information onto each diskette. For example, you have already read that a standard 5.25" diskette has 40 tracks x 9 sectors per track x 512 bytes per sector x 2 side = approx. 360 kb. A high-density 5.25" diskette has 80 tracks x 15 sectors x 512 bytes x 2 sides = approx. 1200 kb or 1.2 Mb.

Each type of diskette reserves space for the boot area, the FAT and the root directory decreasing slightly the space free to store programs and data. Furthermore a system diskette will also contain important system files that reduce the free space even more.

### 1 kb = 1024 bytes

If you do any calculations on storage capacities you may be slightly confused by the numbers not matching up exactly. This is because the computer world is governed by the binary system and 2x2x2x2x2x2x2x2x2x2 = 1024. Thus 1 kb is equated to 1024 bytes and 360 kb therefore becomes 360x1024 = 368 640 bytes.

## Diskette drives

Diskette drives are generally very reliable and you can expect many years of trouble-free performance. There are many diskette drive manufacturers and all drives perform the same task - if one works then it works as well as the next one, such is the nature of digital electronics.

A diskette drive has two functions - recording and retrieving data. However, the individual components involved to carry out these two processes can differ.

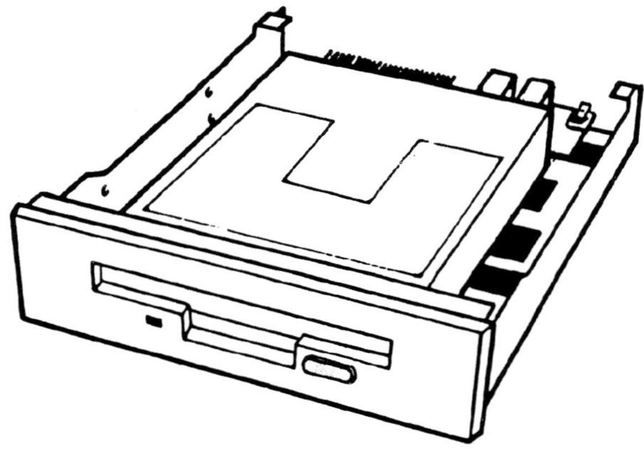

The first thing a drive needs to do is to spin the diskette. This can be done by a belt, more common in older drives, or by direct drive which takes less space and less current. A strobe is used to set the spinning speed accurately.

When the disk is spinning at the correct speed the read/write head must be positioned on the correct track. First however, the head, which can be resting over any of the tracks, is initialised over track 0. Impulses are then sent to a motor to move the head to the desired track.

A stepping motor normally controls this sideways movement. You will often hear a 'clicking' sound coming from your drive as the head is moved in and out. Other techniques are a spring which the motor winds in and out, and a rack and pinion mechanism.

Finally the data is read from the diskette, which may involve stepping over several tracks, and transferred to the computer.

## Controllers

All computers have a controller card that controls the diskette drives, and possibly one or two hard disks as well. This is a card usually taking up an expansion slot in the computer. One or two long flat cables will be seen to loop past the drives, being connected by a connector plug to each drive.

## High-density drives

In the earlier sections about diskette you will have read about high-density diskettes that can store more information than standard diskettes. To be able to use high-density diskette you must have a high-density drive. Standard drives cannot use high-density diskettes. High density drives can, however, use both high-density diskettes and standard diskettes.

## Formatting a diskette

To format a diskette of any size or type the DOS command FORMAT is used. By giving the plain **format** command (e.g. **format a:**) DOS will attempt to format a diskette of the same type as the diskette drive. Thus, if you have a high-density 3.5" drive then DOS will attempt to format the diskette as a high-density 3.5" diskette (1.44 Mb). What if the diskette is not a high-density diskette? This will cause problems.

To overcome such problems, the FORMAT command can be appended with a number of so-called switches that result in unique commands for all combinations of diskettes and drives. The easiest way to present this information is in the form of a table, as follows:

| Drive type | Diskette to format | | | |
|---|---|---|---|---|
| | 5.25" (360 kb) | 5.25" (1.2 Mb) | 3.5" (720 kb) | 3.5" (1.44 Mb) |
| 5.25" | format a: | | | |
| 5.25" HD | format a:/4 | format a: | | |
| 3.5" | | | format a: | |
| 3.5" HD | | | format a:/f:720 | format a: |

The shaded sections denote that it is not possible to format with that combination. Also all occurrences of a: can be replaced with b: if you wish to format a diskette in drive B instead.

From the table it is possible to find some rules, which are now presented together with a few other general points.

- If the drive and diskette to be formatted are of the same type, then it is enough to just type the format command together with the relevant drive letter, e.g **format a:**.
- If the drive is a high-density drive and you wish to format a standard diskette, then you need to modify the format command, e.g. **format a:/4** for 5.25" diskettes, **format b:/f:720** for 3.5" diskettes.
- If you try to format a high-density diskette in a standard disk drive, formatting will not be able to proceed.
- If you try to format a standard diskette in a high-density drive without modifying the format command, formatting will proceed until the diskette runs out of space. You will notice by the noise that the drive is struggling and it is best to cancel the process by pressing **Ctrl + C**, and then re-type the format command.
- To format a system diskette, just add /s to your format command, e.g. **format a:/s** or e.g. **format a:/4/s**.

- To give the diskette a special volume name (up to 11 characters) just add /v to the format command, e.g. **format a:/v** or **format a:/4/s/v**.

# Fault finding

As mentioned earlier, disk drives are generally very reliable and you can expect many years of trouble-free performance. However, they are complex units with sophisticated electronics and mechanical components so if you are inexperienced you should consider leaving any problems to your dealer or another professional person.

Assuming now that you are having problems with a diskette or diskette drive, the following steps will help you to find out where the problem lies.

## Head cleaners

Just as for standard audio tape recorders the read/write head does get dirty. If you have noticed a gradual increase in read/write problems, you should try cleaning the head using one of the readily available head cleaning diskettes.

## Is it the diskette or the drive unit?

Try out several diskettes - if all of them cause problems then the drive unit is probably faulty and you can continue with the next test or call your repair man.

If only your original diskette causes the problem then you should suspect that you have a faulty diskette. In this case you will have to decide how important the information stored on the diskette was. If it was of no great importance, or easily replaced, then just throw it away. If it is more important you will need the help of a suitable software like *Norton Utilities* to help you restore the lost data - if it is possible. You could also choose to send the diskette to a data recovery agency.

## Is it the drive unit or the computer?

The next stage is to test the drive unit. To do this you will need to replace the suspected unit with another drive unit. If you have two drives, then you can swap them around. If you only have one you will need to borrow one from a friend or possibly a dealer who trusts you. Physically exchanging drives is not so complicated as you may think:

- Turn off the power supply to your computer and UNPLUG it. Never take the following steps if the computer is connected to the mains.

---

*Warning!*
*Do not proceed with the following steps unless you have disconnected your computer from the power supply.*

---

- Unscrew and remove the outer casing.
- Locate the faulty disk drive and remove the retaining screws along its side.
- The disk drive will have two cables connected to it at the back. Draw the unit gently out a little, usually forwards, note how the two cables are connected and unplug them.
- Remove the drive completely.
- Install the replacement drive, following the instructions in the opposite order.

Now it's time to re-test the drive and diskette. If the problem goes away then you know that the original drive was faulty, and you can send it for repair. If the problem still exists then you know that the fault lies in the computer itself and you should have the whole computer looked at by an expert.

## ASSIGN sorts out mixed diskette problem

The last problem in this chapter is highlighted by the following situation:

- Your system has two diskette drives, a 5.25" drive as drive A, and a 3.5" drive as drive B. A friend or work mate comes to you and asks you to install a program he/she has on a 3.5" diskette.

The problem is that this program must be installed from drive A (not an uncommon requirement), but on your system the 3.5" drive is drive B. What do you do?

You could answer "*Sorry I'm just off to an important meeting with ...*"

You could set about copying the contents of the 3.5" diskette onto a 5.25" diskette, hoping that the program is not copy protected in any way.

There is an easier method - the ASSIGN command - which allows you to temporarily rename a drive. Try this (if your computer has two diskette drives):

- **If you have a diskette based system** put your DOS diskette in drive A.
- Type:

  ```
  assign a=b
  ```

- Press the ↵ key.
- Put any diskette with some files on in drive B.
- Type:

  ```
  dir a:
  ```

- Press the ↵ key.

You will notice that the directory of the diskette in drive B is listed despite the fact that you gave the command dir a:. In other words the **assign a = b** command has instructed DOS to treat drive B as if it were drive A.

To restore the situation so that A is A and B is B do as follows:

- Type:

  ```
  assign
  ```

- Press the ↵ key.

If you turn off your computer, then the next time you start it the drives will also behave normally, ASSIGN is only a temporary command.

So to solve the stated problem you would take the following steps:

1. Issue the **assign a = b** command.
2. Install the program using the 3.5" B drive, which is temporarily acting as drive A.
3. Issue the assign command to restore the drives to their normal designations.
4. Await the approval and wonder of the person who came to you to do the job!

# 5. Hard Disks

This chapter takes a closer look at the workings and problems of a hard disk. Many terms and phrases are explained, but it is assumed that you know about the root directory and subdirectories and the DOS commands MD, CD and RD, used to create, change and delete subdirectories. If you have not yet reached this level, then you should consider reading our earlier book called **PC Crash Course and Survival Guide** by the same author.

To put you in a good mood to start with you should know that one day your hard disk will crash, that is it will be damaged or stop functioning altogether, along with some or all of the information stored on it. So just make sure that you know enough about backing up your data, that is taking suitable copies of anything that is important - the very last section in this book will advise you on making back-up copies. A good tip is also to make sure that you have a system diskette at the ready - if, one day, your computer (assuming it has a hard disk) doesn't boot, or start, you may still be able to start it with your system diskette and even gain access to valuable files and continue working. See more about this in the section **Problems - Computer will not boot**.

## Closed units

In many ways, a hard disk is like a floppy disk or diskette. It has the same boot record, FAT, root directory and data area (see previous chapter for more details on these). Rather than being a single disc, a hard disk is a closed unit housing several discs and many read/write heads. The unit is sealed to keep out dust which would affect the high precision workings.

## Mass storage

The first hard disks could store no more than 5 or 10 Mb, which at the time was considered to be a lot. These days you cannot even buy such small hard disks, and some larger programs are so large that they would not fit onto such disks at all.

Hard disks have become mass storage units - 20 Mb, 30 Mb, 40 Mb, 70 Mb, 100 Mb, 300 Mb, 650 Mb are some examples of storage capacities. A 650 Mb hard disk is capable of storing the equivalent of over 300 000 standard text pages - that's some book! Why should anyone need such a large storage capacity? Obviously such a hard disk would be useful if shared by several users as in a network, for example. Graphics also often require large storage areas - a typical picture may use anything up to 1 Mb of storage space. A 40 Mb disk with perhaps 20 Mb free for storing pictures would soon be filled.

The larger the hard disk, the more you stand to lose when it crashes!

## Access times

One of the major developments of hard disks is the average access time. This is the average time it takes to access any data anywhere on the disk and has become an important part of the overall performance of a computer system. Slower hard disks will have an average access time of around 65 ms (65 milliseconds, or 65/1000 of a second). Medium fast hard disks have access times of around 40 ms while faster hard disks take under 30 ms. This figure is continually being improved upon.

How does the average access time affect you? If you are using a program that does not read from or write to the hard disk, then the speed of the hard disk will only affect how fast the program is loaded in the first place - it may make a difference of a few seconds. On the other hand, a program that writes to and reads from the hard disk during its execution will be affected each and every time such an operation occurs. A slower hard disk here will keep you waiting a second or two longer each time.

The overall performance of the hard disk is, however, not solely a matter of access speeds. The so-called interleave and the rate of data transfer to the processor both play an important role.

### Interleaves

Imagine that your computer needs to pick up some data from a single track on the hard disk. This track, and every other track, is divided into a number of sectors, typically seventeen. The fact is that a hard disk spins so fast that the computer cannot keep up with it. Reading the sectors one after the other as they spin past is too much for all but the fastest systems.

Let's assume that for each spin of the disk the computer can cope with reading one sector. Thus, to read all seventeen sectors, it would take seventeen disk revolutions, and the interleave factor is 17:1. Let's assume now that the computer can manage to read 5 sectors per revolution - interleave factor 5:1 - this would mean that four revolutions were necessary to read all 17 sectors. Reading every other sector (interleave factor 2:1) would require only 2 revolutions, the first revolution reading sectors 1, 3, 5, etc., with the second revolution reading sectors 2, 4, etc.

A standard PC with an 8088 processor will typically have an interleave factor of 5:1, an AT a factor of 3:1. Changing the interleave factor is a way of tuning your hard disk performance to that of your computer, but not something for the beginner to tamper with!

## Interface standards and Controller cards

The interface is the means of transferring the data read from a hard disk to the computer itself. It is known as a *Controller card*, and is an add-in card that is installed in the computer. All hard disks (and diskette drives) need a controller card.

The standard used from the beginning has been the ST-506/412, which transfers data at a rate of 5 million bits per second (5 Mbits/sec). Even if this sounds a lot it is not considered fast enough for the most powerful applications. In recent years other standards have been developed; SCSI (Small Computer System Interface) that manages 12 megabits per second (Mbits/se)c and ESDI (Enhanced Small Device Interface) which can manage up to 20 Mbits/sec.

If you buy a computer with a hard disk it will already be in place. If you buy a separate hard disk you will probably need a controller card too. However, some computers will already have a controller card with unused hard disk connectors in which case it is simply a matter of plugging in the hard disk. Make sure that the hard disk and the controller card are of the same type!

### MFM and RLL

MFM (Modified Frequency Modulation) is the standard technique used for storing data on a disk. RLL (Run Length Limited) is a more recent technique for storing data that increases the capacity by up to 50%. It enables each track to be divided into 26 sectors instead of the normal 17. This increase affects the interleave ratio because the sectors are more tightly packed.

Some companies have started selling separate RLL hard disk controller cards, but be warned... It is not just a matter of replacing your standard MFM controller card with an RLL card and expecting a 50% increase. Because RLL increases the quantity of data stored it also needs a higher quality disk and most standard disks will not satisfy this need.

## The 32 Mb limit

The rapid increase in storage capacities has caused problems. DOS was limited to using 32 Mb hard disks, although from DOS version 4.0 and later this limit has now been increased to 512 Mb.

### Partitions

If you have a DOS version earlier than 4.0 and a large hard disk, the hard disk must be divided into smaller units called partitions. For example, a 60 Mb hard disk may divided up into two drives (C: and D:) each 30 Mb. Thus, even though you only physically have one hard disk in your computer, the computer treats it as two separate hard disks.

Partitioning is done with the DOS command FDISK. Many computer dealers configure hard disks for you so that you will not need to use FDISK. If not, you will need to check out your DOS manual.

## Hard disk cards

A hard disk card is an add-in card that is a hard disk and controller card all in one. It is a simple way of adding a hard disk to your computer, but will often take up a lot of room inside the computer. It requires a free expansion slot and will probably encroach upon the space for the adjacent card.

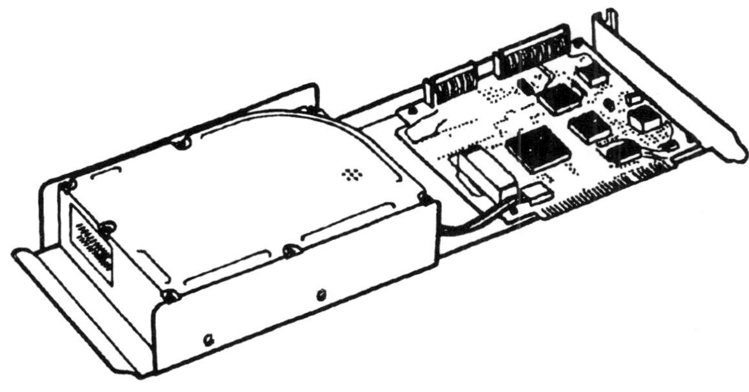

## Menu programs

The large storage capacity of a hard disk means that you can store a large amount of files. A 40 Mb disk, for example, could typically store 2000 files. These files will be spread out over subdirectories, subsubdirectories and subsubsubdirectories, etc. Using DOS commands to move around the subdirectories can be a tiring experience, even if you remember exactly how you have organised your hard disk.

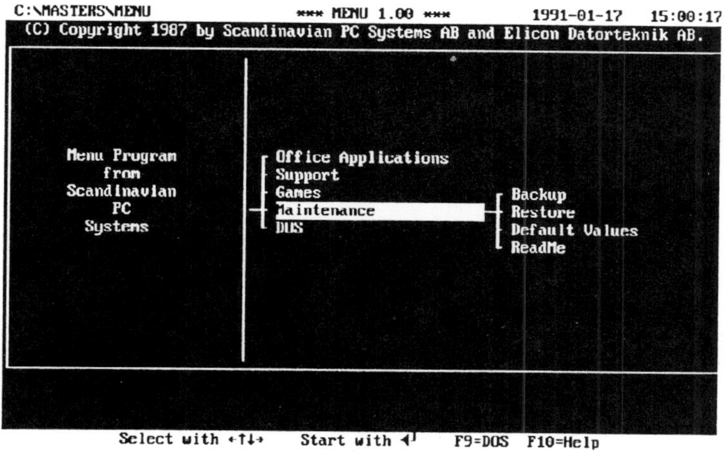

There are two simple ways of making life easier for yourself - batch files and menu programs. Batch files involve storing series of DOS commands in a single file. Running the batch file then carries out the DOS commands saving you the bother. Batch files have been covered in depth in an earlier chapter.

A menu program allows you to build up a picture of your hard disk as you wish to see it. You create a menu and each option is given its own set of DOS commands to follow. You can divide your programs into menus and submenus irrespective of how they are physically stored on your disk. Here's an example:

To start your word processor you simply select the Word Processor option in the menu, easy and free of problems. A menu program could be the most useful and most used program on your hard disk!

## Problems

The remainder of this chapter is dedicated to problems you may have with your hard disk including *fragmentation* that results in a considerable drop in performance.

For virtually all problems that occur you will need the help of a special program to assist you in solving the problem. Examples of such programs are PC Tools and Norton Utilities, others exist too.

### Computer does not boot from hard disk

If you turn on your computer (assuming you have a hard disk) and it refuses to start, then you have a serious problem. It may be caused by a DOS system file or the COMMAND.COM file being corrupt or even the CONFIG.SYS or AUTOEXEC.BAT files trying to run a corrupt file. Whatever the cause you cannot start your computer or access your files.

In such a case you will need a system diskette. By inserting the diskette in drive A and re-starting the computer you should at least get things going. When the `A:>`prompt is displayed you can try to access the hard disk:

- Type:

  `c:`

If this does not succeed and you are faced with the message `Invalid drive specification` you have problems, and should seek the help of a knowledgeable person or try Norton Utilities (or a similar program) which is a software package specifically designed for data recovery and disk management. You could as a temporary measure check the cables from the controller card to the hard disk to see that they have not loosened.

If you successfully get the `c:>` prompt you should rename the AUTOEXEC.BAT and CONFIG.SYS files and try rebooting the computer to see if the fault lies here. Use the following commands:

**ren config.sys cfg.sys**
**ren autoexec.bat ae.bat**

If the computer successfully reboots then you know that the problem comes from one of these two files. If not then a DOS message, sometimes displayed when starting the computer, may help you.

`Non-system disk` suggests that the system files on your hard disk may have been damaged. Run the DOS command SYS to re-copy these to your hard disk as follows:

- Start your computer with a system diskette and then insert your DOS diskette in drive A.

- Type:

  `sys c:`

`Bad or Missing Command Interpreter` - this message implies that the system file COMMAND.COM is missing or has been damaged. Proceed as follows:

- Start your computer with a system diskette and then insert your DOS diskette in drive A.

- Type:

  `copy command.com c:\`

If none of these solve the problem then you really need Norton Utilities or other suitable help.

## Hard disk slowing down - fragmentation

When DOS saves your files on disk, it does not automatically save them as one long unit. Generally speaking, each file is divided into smaller units that fill one sector each on the hard disk. DOS will then fill in unused sectors anywhere on the disk so that one file may be spread out over a number of undetached sectors. From the beginning files will be saved in one long run, but as you save, overwrite and delete files more and more "holes" will appear on the disk and future files will be split - this is called fragmentation.

The net result of fragmentation is a slower hard disk. To read in a fragmented file the read/write head will have to be repositioned several times, so you will even hear the effects of loading and writing fragmented files.

## Compression/Optimization

The cure for fragmentation is disk compression or optimization. You can buy a program, like **PC Tools**, that will reorganize your disk for you. It will read all the files on the disk and re-save them so that each file is stored as one long string of data on the disk, thus restoring data transfer speeds to their highest rate.

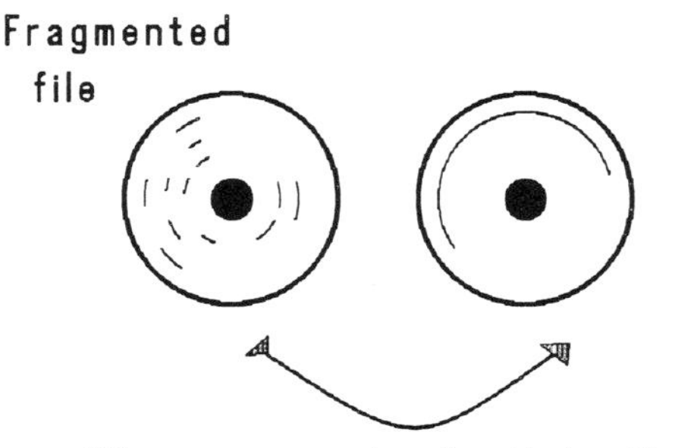


Disk compression is a quick and simple process and highly recommended for any serious hard disk user.

## Accidentally erased files

One thing that every computer user does at least once in his life is to mistakenly erase a wanted file or group of files. Erased files are often recoverable. Several programs are available that will help you to recover deleted files - PC Tools and Norton Utilities being two of the most popular.

When you erase a file DOS does not actually delete the data from the disk, it only replaces the first letter of the filename in the directory listing to mark the fact that the file is no longer in use. However, DOS will at some point use the freed space to save other files at which point the old deleted file is truly lost. If you discover that you have erased the wanted file early enough, you may well be able to recover it. To give yourself as much chance as possible of saving the file STOP WORKING with your computer - each time a file is saved you run the risk of deleting the old file for ever. Then run a file recovery program.

## Accidentally formatted diskette

Sorry you're out of luck here. If you have accidentally formatted a diskette that contained vital data by using the DOS command FORMAT then the whole of the data area will have been wiped out.

Norton Utilities has a program called SF (Safe Format) that allows you to format diskettes without destroying the data area. Using this instead of the normal DOS command will mean that you can recover data from a re-formatted diskette. PC Tools offers a similar program PCFORMAT.

## Accidentally formatted hard disk

Believe it or not there is a chance of recovering from an accidentally formatted hard disk, something that is a real threat for users with earlier DOS versions (later DOS versions will not format a hard disk without the disk name C:, D:, etc. being given, thus minimising the risk of accidental format).

Again you should turn to PC Tools, Norton Utilities or a similar program.

### Read/write errors

Read/write errors occur when a sector has a bad CRC (Cyclic Redundancy Check). When information is written to a diskette a special checksum value is calculated and stored along with the data itself. When the data is read at a later date a new checksum is also calculated. The new checksum is compared with the checksum stored for that sector. If the two checksums do not match up then the data that was read from the disk is not the same as the data that was stored on the disk - a read error has occurred.

Most often this will mean that the program is unusable. If it is a data file you may or may not be able to salvage some of the data. Again PC Tools/Norton Utilities will be needed.

### Other problems

Here are some other problems that may be helped with PC Tools or Norton Utilities. Furthermore, **Appendix C Some Common DOS Error Messages** provide answers to some more problems.

`Bad FAT`. If a program reports a bad FAT then it is useful to know that DOS actually keeps a copy of the FAT, and you may be able to save the disk by utilising the copy.

`Unable to read drive`. Sometimes a disk is so badly damaged that reading files is impossible. Recovering from this is time consuming and often only partially possible.

## Back-ups

This final section provides an easy guide to taking a full and comprehensive back-up of a complete hard disk. This will normally take a long time and a lot of diskettes. For example 20 Mb of data on a hard disk will require over 50 standard 360 kb diskettes or approximately 20 high-density 1.2 Mb diskettes.

If you have a lot of important data that needs backing up often you should invest in a special back-up program (e.g. PC Tools or Fastback) or a tape back-up unit. There is no excuse for not having a back-up of important data files because you know that one day something WILL go wrong with your hard disk.

There is a DOS command, called BACKUP, that will do a back-up for you. It is possible to select certain files only for backing up and thereby greatly reducing the time and number of diskettes needed. Here are the necessary instructions for carrying out a full back-up (for more details see your DOS manual):

- Work out how many diskettes you need - they must be formatted before proceeding.
- Type the following command:

```
backup c: a: /s
```

Now follow the back-up procedure and change diskettes as necessary. It is important to carefully number the diskettes in order.

If you ever need to use your back-up diskettes, you should refer to your DOS manual or appendix D at the back of this book, the command RESTORE is used.

# 6. Printers

Printing is one of the main goals for computer users. Letters, accounts, graphs and pictures are some examples of why we use computers at all, so how to produce the final result becomes very important. In this chapter the different types of printers will be discussed briefly along with the most common printer problems that occur.

## Types of printers

There are basically five types of printer:

- Dot matrix
  Daisy-wheel
  Ink jet
  Laser
  Plotter

Daisy-wheel printers are fast disappearing and not covered in the following explanations. They are of interest if your only need is for quality letter printing at a rock bottom price. They are slow, very noisy and cannot print graphics, but give quality letter printout as good as any typewriter and can be found at bargain prices.

### Dot matrix printers

The most common and least expensive type of printer is the dot matrix printer. This works by hammering pins against a ribbon and the paper in such a pattern as to form the necessary characters.

There are several interesting points to note; the printing speed, the quality of the printout, the available types of printout and the standards it can emulate.

The printing speed is always quoted in characters per second, but this speed relates to the top speed that the printer can reach. In effect the average printing speed will be much lower when line breaks and the stop and start movements are taken into account. Thus a reasonably cheap dot matrix printer with a quoted print speed of 80 cps (characters per second) may only manage 40 on average.

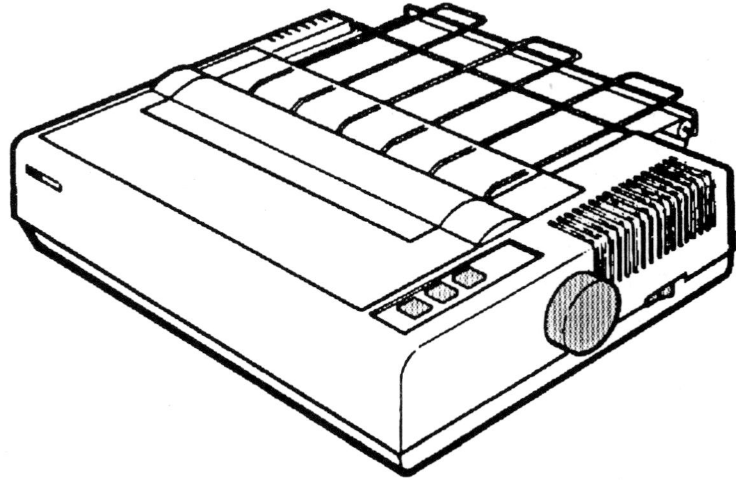

A golden rule is; the higher the printing speed the higher the price. Some dot matrix printers have two or three printing heads thus increasing the printing speed up to 600 to 800 cps.

The print quality is determined by the actual design of the printer and the number of pins used in the printing head. Many printers use 9 pins to form each character, while a more expensive standard of printer uses 24 pins. It is easy to guess which is the more expensive, but you really can see the difference.

Dot matrix printers can normally print in compressed style (a smaller print than the standard), expanded style (double width print) and near letter quality (NLQ). NLQ printing gives a much better quality printout and slows the printing down considerably. More expensive printers offer even more possibilities.

As far as standards go, there are two important ones to note - one for text and one for graphics. The IBM Proprinter is such an important standard that virtually all dot matrix printers can emulate this standard, and virtually all software that uses a printer can be set-up for this standard. A similar standard exists for printing graphics - here the standard is EPSON FX. Dot matrix printers, are however, not ideally suited to graphics giving slow and low quality printouts especially for solid black areas.

Many printers can also emulate other printers and even have their own "mode" or character set, but this is not definitely an advantage - for the user with more simple needs it is probably better to install the printer and programs to use the IBM standard.

Colour dot matrix printers are now available.

Dot matrix printers are relatively cheap, but... do not buy a matrix printer if you need a quiet printer. In a library they will disturb readers, in a hospital they will disturb patients, in a professional office they will disturb everybody and at home they will wake the baby. For high quality graphics, real letter quality or desk top publishing (DTP) a dot matrix falls short of the mark although some 24 pin printers may be acceptable for some - look at a laser or an ink-jet printer.

## Laser printers

If dot matrix printers give slow low quality printouts as a rule, then laser printers give high speed, top quality printouts. Laser printers are the best printers available and have the highest price tag. Laser printers also have the same important aspects; speed, quality, variation and standards.

Laser printers print a whole page at a time. The speed of a laser printer is judged by the number of completed sheets it can turn out per minute. Typical "slow" lasers produce 6 pages per minute (ppm) others 8ppm, 10ppm or even more. The printing speed is, however, dependent on

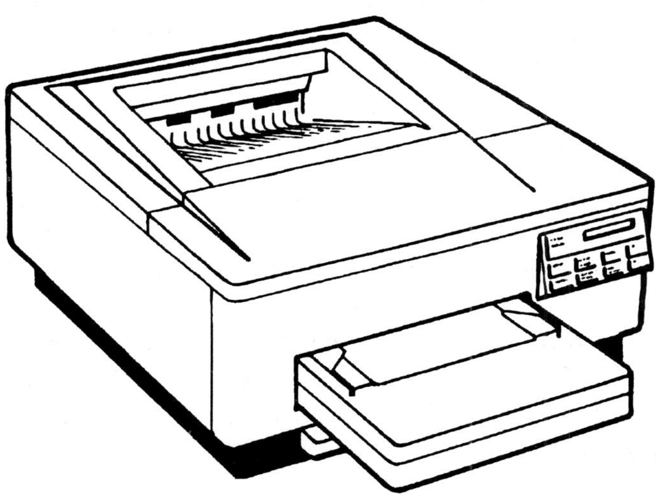

what you are printing - a page containing a large picture may take several minutes to print.

The quality of a laser printout is measured by the dots per inch (dpi) printed - like the dot matrix printer the laser printer in fact prints just a lot of dots! Most laser printers print at 300 dpi, thus a square inch will contain 300 x 300 = 90 000 dots. It is common these days to print manuals and even books using a laser printout at 300 dpi, the quality being perfectly acceptable so that only somebody "in the business" would deem the final product be of a low-quality. There are laser printers that can print at 400 dpi almost doubling the quality of the final printout. One system at least can print at 1000 dpi, which is gives a quality marginally lower than typesetting in the traditional manner. Of course, quality costs!

There are two important standards for laser printers; HP Laser Jet and HP Graphics Language (from Hewlett Packard) and PostScript. With HP Laser Jet compatible laser printers you get a few standard typefaces that can print in a few different sizes, but can add special cartridges or typeface programs to extend the range of printing possibilities. High quality graphics can also be printed.

### PostScript and laser printers

PostScript is a special page description language that can be used to print text and graphics. The characters that can be printed are scaleable. This means that rather than storing a copy of each character in different sizes as a pattern of dots, each character is described by the way it is formed. Thus the characters can be printed at any size, within the limits set by the printer. PostScript printers are often supplied with 35 different typefaces and others can be installed through special typeface programs.

The main difference between a HP and PostScript laser lies not in the quality, both print at 300 dpi, but in the flexibility of PostScript. PostScript printers typically cost twice as much as HP compatible printers, but offer much more.

Colour laser printers are now available.

### Ink-jet printers

Ink-jet printers lie somewhere between dot matrix and laser printers. The quality is nearly as high as that of a laser printer and the price much lower. Ink-jet printers are quiet, cheap alternatives to dot matrix printers. The quality of the printout depends on how many dots are squirted onto the paper, rather like the number of pins in the printing head of a dot matrix.

Print speeds are comparable to dot matrix print speeds and thus much slower than laser printers. Unfortunately some ink-jet printers have their own standards, although many can emulate the all-important IBM Proprinter and EPSON standards. If you are considering buying such a ink-jet printer you must therefore check the standards each printer make can emulate, and check your software to see which standards it can be set up to use.

Colour ink jet printers are now available.

### Plotters

Plotters are a different sort of printing mechanism often associated with CAD/CAM and other drawing programs. The important difference is that plotters actually use pens that are steered around the paper to produce real lines rather than patterns of dots.

A typical plotter may have four, six or eight different colour pens. The higher the resolution the better the quality of the printout. Printing speed is also important as full page drawings can take a long time to be printed.

Finally, in the world of plotters, HP GL (Hewlett Packard Graphics Language) is the standard - the very same standard as used in some laser printers.

## Printer standards and control codes

The last few pages has involved some talk of standards - here's why they are so important...

Let us assume that you wish to print the words "a million" in bold text. Apart from sending the actual words to the printer, the printer must be told that bold type is requested. Thus prior to the actual words a control code is sent to set up the printer for bold typing. The actual words are then sent and printed. Finally a new control code will be sent to the printer to mark the end of the bold printing. It is these control codes that constitute a standard.

For example, the IBM Proprinter standard requires two code numbers to activate bold type - 27 and then 69. Code number 27 is very special and represents Escape, this informs the printer that a control code is coming rather than ordinary text. 69 is the code number to start bold printing. After this the text "a million" is sent and printed. Finally the control numbers to end bold printing, 27 and 70, are sent to the printer. The IBM Proprinter standard covers a set of pre-defined control number sequences to control the printer.

Normally your word processor, or other program you are using, sends the necessary control codes to your printer. You will have marked a certain block of text as bold, for example, and the program does the rest. If your program is set up for a different standard it will probably send a completely different control code for bold printing, which will produce anything except the desired result!

See also the section called **Garbage**.

## Connecting a printer

A printer can be connected to your computer in two ways; via a parallel port or via a serial port. Some printers provide both sorts of port, others only one type. Your printer may or may not have a free serial port. If you have the choice, then you should connect your printer to a parallel port - it is less trouble setting up and gives faster printing.

Each character that is sent to the printer comprises eight single bits which need to be sent. With a parallel port there are 8 data lines available so all eight bits can be sent in one go. With a serial connection there is only one data line available so the bits have to be sent one at a time, one after the other.

The command needed to re-direct the printout from the parallel port LPT1 to the serial port COM1 is as follows:

**mode lpt1: = com1:**

If necessary you should edit the AUTOEXEC.BAT file to correct this problem. This is easily done using your word processor in its ASCII mode (or text only)

*Note:*
*If you have a diskette only system, you will need to copy the DOS program MODE.COM onto your system diskette to enable these commands to be carried out.*

## Page breaks

A common problem for beginners is that they cannot get the page breaks to match the paper. The problem here, which is mostly related to dot matrix printers, is that both the printer and the program involved need to know what size of paper is being used.

Normally the paper size is set in a printing options set up menu somewhere in the program you are using. Not unsurprisingly this MUST correspond to the actual size of paper you are using. Here are some of the most common types of paper lengths:

| Paper length or type | |
|---|---|
| 11 inches | |
| A4 | |
| 12 inches | |

How many lines each type of paper has room for depends on the line spacing of the printer, the two most common being 6 lines per inch and 8 lines per inch. Printing at 6 lines per inch gives the following number of lines available:

| Paper length or type | No. of lines |
|---|---|
| 11 inches | 66 lines |
| A4 | 70 lines |
| 12 inches | 72 lines |

Thus the program must be set for the number of printing lines available.

*Note:*
*Some programs, usually in combination with laser printers, require the actual paper type or the actual size of the paper in inches or centimetres to be specified. With such set-ups the page break problem does not normally occur.*

## Graphics and other special characters

Sometimes a certain character will be displayed on the screen but not printed, this is more likely to be true for graphics characters and other special characters. Several things can cause such a phenomena.

Firstly there are some characters which are not printable. If you check the ASCII table in appendix A at the back of this book, you will see that characters below number 32 are not there. These lower values in the table are used to control printers, a code is needed for each function such as backspacing, new paragraphs, new pages, tabs, etc. However, even though these lower number codes do each have a symbol to represent them and some word processors and other programs can even display them on the screen. Even so, if you type in character number 3, which is represented by a heart (if your word processor can display it at all, printing will result in all but a heart.

Another reason for not getting the standard IBM graphics characters may be that you have your printer set up to use another standard. Dot matrix printers often have a mode that only prints the characters up to number 127 in the ASCII table, or even their own mode with a different character set altogether. Your printer handbook will explain the different modes or emulations available and list any different character sets it has - check to see how your printer is installed, and what characters such an installation provides.

## Bold type and other printer effects not working properly

If you have problems trying to get some printer effects working, for example double underlining or bold italics or even Times Roman 24pt italic, then first check that your printer is capable of producing the desired type. Just because you have a word processor that allows you to do bold italics, it doesn't mean that your printer is capable of producing that style.

HP Laser Jet compatibles are another example - you can, for example, choose a Times Roman (or Dutch) font with a size of 12pts in normal, italic, bold or bold italic. Larger sizes, however, are limited to bold, not even normal or italic.

When you are sure that your printer can cope but doesn't, you should check that both the printer and program are set up to use the same mode or emulation. Even if most things seem to work, a difference in the two set-ups might just result in bold italic underlined not working because different control codes are required for this combination.

## Problems with PostScript printers

Most PostScript type laser printers do not have a standard ASCII character set, but another standard for the PostScript language. Although all of the letters have the same codes as for the ASCII table, nearly all of the graphics and special characters are replaced with another set - see appendix A for a listing of the PostScript character set.

Thus using a word processor and other programs and doing something with graphics characters, e.g. boxes, may well cause a real problem. Different word processors handle things in different ways. Even with my own PostScript printer set up to emulate a HP laser printer I cannot get the graphics characters using Microsoft Word because the printer just does not have them stored. Doing the same thing with Word Perfect works fine, however, because that program sends its own character set to the printer, thus enabling it to print these characters.

## Laser margins

Laser printers have restrictions as to how close to the end of the paper they can print. Unfortunately most of them leave a slightly wider right-hand margin than left-hand. The unsuspecting user will then try to centre his beautiful piece of work bang in the middle of the page. It was set up perfectly on the screen, but the different margin restrictions of the printer put everything off line! Oh well, just move it a bit in the photocopier!

## Garbage

A final word for those of you who mix up the standards - garbage! Don't settle for anything less. If you type in a few sentences and set up your word processor to print on a PostScript printer, and then set up the printer as HP Laser Jet compatible, your few sentences will be turned into endless pages of the PostScript programming language - sheer garbage to anyone but the initiated PostScript programmer. Try the reverse situation and print a HP Laser Jet file on a PostScript printer and you probably will not get even a squeak out of the printer, at least saving on the paper. That's the way it is with mixed standards.

# 7. Keyboards, Mice and Other Input Devices

One of the main functions of a computer is the input of data, or information. If you never put anything into your computer then it will have a hard time producing anything for you! By far the most common means of data input is the keyboard as virtually all computers have one. However, there are other methods and some of these will be covered briefly in this chapter. You will also find a more in-depth look at the keyboard and the mouse including some of the problems related to their use in your day-to-day contact with computers.

## The keyboard

The keyboard is the most common way to put data into your computer, so what happens when you press a key? What can go wrong with a keyboard? What are scan codes and buffers? Read on!

### Scan codes

Your keyboard effectively constitutes a grid system as depicted in the diagram below.

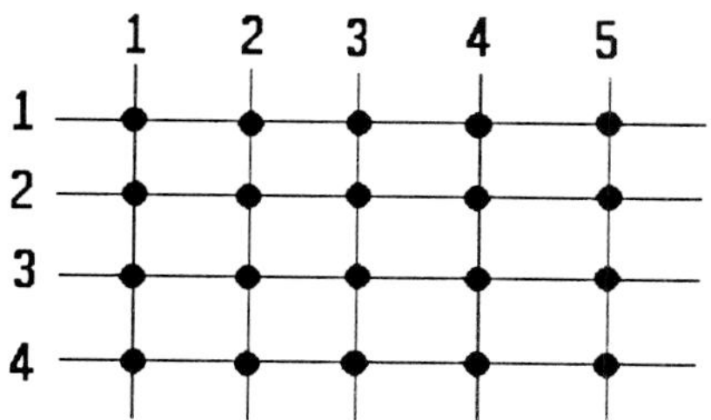

Each key has its own point in the grid with a vertical and a horizontal axis. Each time you hit a key, the unique reference point, or scan code, is passed on to the computer.

### Buffer

Within the keyboard is a small buffer where information on your key depressions, the scan codes, is temporarily held. Scan codes are not automatically sent to the computer processor - they are picked up by the computer as required. Thus the keyboard buffer can sometimes get full when the computer is busy doing some other task and not looking for key depressions. If you press a key when the keyboard buffer is already full, you should get the familiar beep.

## KEYB and KEYBUK - Keyboard mapping programs

One of the most common problems a computer user is faced with involves the keyboard. Most often users in different countries have trouble typing specific characters such as their own unique national characters, or symbols other than letters and numbers. The basic explanation is quite simple; all personal computers are manufactured to run using a standard USA keyboard.

Of course there is a way around this so that the British can have their £ sign, the French their áàéè and the Scandinavians their öäå. If you're not using a USA keyboard, your computer needs to load a very special keyboard program - a DOS command - to adapt it to the standard of your country.

This special DOS command will normally be automatically loaded each time you start your computer, so that you don't have to think about it anymore. When you install DOS on your hard disk, or create a DOS system diskette for the first time, you will be guided through the process of choosing your country, and a special file will be created to load the keyboard program.

There are two versions of this DOS command as described below:

#### KEYB

The DOS command KEYB installs a national keyboard with the help of a layout file, normally called KEYBOARD.SYS. The command is followed by a space and a two letter code to identify the country, e.g. KEYB UK, KEYB IT, KEYB FR, etc.

KEYB is used in DOS versions 3.3 and later and replaces the older command (see below) KEYBUK, KEYBIT, etc. The KEYB command should be placed in your AUTOEXEC.BAT file.

### KEYBUK

The KEYBUK command is used to install the U.K. keyboard in DOS versions prior to 3.3. The KEYBUK command should be placed in your AUTOEXEC.BAT file.

# Keyboard problems

In this section you can read about the most common problems caused by keyboards.

## Keyboards can go wrong

Keyboards are generally very reliable, but can of course go wrong. Generally speaking, if your keyboard has been working and suddenly goes wrong, there is not much you can do more than replace it or send it for a service. The keen DIY man (or woman) may be able to repair or replace a damaged or sticking key, but that's about all.

Before making any decisions there is an easy test to try: borrow another keyboard from a friend and see if that works correctly. If it does then you know that it is your keyboard that is damaged. If your friends keyboard does not work either, then you should suspect some problem with the main computer unit itself, in which case you will need a proper service technician.

## PC/AT switch

A little known problem that can arise, especially if you replace a keyboard or system unit, is a switch on the keyboard itself. A few keyboards have a switch to select a PC or AT (i.e. 286, 386 or 486) machine. This switch is usually on the underside of the keyboard and if wrongly selected the keys will not match.

## Symbols do not match keys

Having loaded the keyboard program KEYB or KEYBUK (automatically or manually), the unique national characters do not usually present a problem. The main problem is that the keyboard program doesn't always match the keys, for example, the symbols such as \{[]}, etc. When you press the asterisk key * you may see a + and the backslash key produces anything but the all-important backslash.

In simple terms, a keyboard program re-maps the standard USA keyboard to suit you own country standard, but the keyboard you have may not necessarily completely match the keyboard programs' standard. That's the way standards work in the wonderful world of computers.

The unique national characters work, but some of the other symbols don't match up. What do I do?

One possibility is to check the diskettes and instructions delivered with your computer. Sometimes a replacement KEYBUK file is supplied that will solve the problem for you.

### The Alt key solution

All characters and symbols that a computer can display, whether they be French, Scandinavian or other oddities, have been given a special code number. Their is a special table for IBM compatible computers, called the ASCII table, which lists each character and symbol together with its unique code number. The complete table is presented in at the back of this book in Appendix A.

A special key, the **Alt** key, can be used to produce any character or symbol, irrespective of where the character/symbol is to be found on the keyboard, if at all.

- First look up the code number for the character/symbol you wish to produce.
- Depress the **Alt** key and, using the numerical keypad on the right-hand side of the keyboard, type the code number.
- Release the **Alt** key and the desired character/symbol should be displayed.

*Note:*
*You must use the numerical keypad on the right-hand side of your keyboard. This system will not work using the line of number keys above the letters.*

You should be warned that some application programs may not allow you to produce all of the characters, and even this method may fail.

### Example 1a

You are using your word processor to write a letter to a Swede who lives at Glasvägen 3. Quite, they've got that funny a with two dots over it. If you check the ASCII table in Appendix A, you will find that ä has the code number 132. When you get to the ä, which is not on your keyboard, do the following:

Depress the Alt key and, using the numerical keypad on the right-hand side of the keyboard.

- Type:

  `132`

- Release the **Alt** key and an ä should be displayed.

### Other solutions

There are other ways of re-mapping a keyboard. One is with the help of a special program, e.g. **Prokey**, that allows you to re-program any key to produce any character or even a sequence of characters. Thus for example, you could re-define the function keys to draw graphics characters or re-define any other key which does not match up with your keyboard. This type of program is always memory resident and takes up some of your computer's memory. There may also be problems with other memory resident programs.

Another method is to use DOS to re-define certain keys. This is a bit more complicated and is not covered in this book.

# The Mouse

The mouse has become a very important computer accessory and in some cases, desk top publishing and drawing programs, it has become a necessity. It provides a quick method of moving the cursor around the screen, for marking areas and blocks of text, and for selecting options presented in a menu.

## Different standards

Needless to say there are different standards. However, one standard stands out - Microsoft Mouse. All programs that can use a mouse can be used with at least one type of mouse, i.e. Microsoft Mouse, and often several other types. That does not mean that you must have a Microsoft Mouse - many other mice can emulate (act like) a Microsoft Mouse.

## Serial and Bus connections

There are three ways of connecting a mouse to your computer as described below.

### Special mouse port

Some more recent computers are supplied with a special mouse port as a part of their design. In such cases it is a simple matter of connecting a mouse to the port.

### Serial port

Perhaps the most common way of connecting a mouse is via a serial port. Most computers have one or two serial ports and if one serial port is free, then you can simply plug in a mouse. One reason for not doing so would be if you are intending to install a modem, printer or other accessory that will use the spare port.

### Bus mouse

If you have no free serial port you can install a bus mouse. Such a package will include both a mouse and an add-in card that you will have to install yourself. In doing so you will have to get slightly technical because installing a bus mouse involves knowing a little about IRQs.

As you have read earlier, your computer checks the keyboard to see if any scan codes are waiting in the keyboard buffer (as a result of key depressions). In the same way the computer must be able to know if a mouse has been moved or a button pressed. To cope with this your computer has several special "lines" called IRQs (Interrupt ReQuests) along which a bus mouse and other accessories including serial and parallel ports, hard disk and diskette drives. Each such IRQ line is numbered, and installing a bus mouse card involves choosing a free unreserved number. This process is described in the instructions that come with such a package.

## Mouse drivers

Finally, having physically installed a mouse you must inform the computer that the mouse exists and involves loading a special program called a mouse driver. This is done using the CONFIG.SYS or AUTOEXEC.BAT file. Again the process is described in the instructions that come with such a package.

## Application programs and mice

It is worth stating that not all programs can be used with mice. If the program is not made for use with a mouse, then installing a mouse will have no effect on the program.

Programs that do use a mouse will often have a set-up procedure where you need to select the type of mouse you have. A few programs that use a mouse will just assume that you have a Microsoft mouse.

## Mouse actions

Apart from moving the mouse around to move a pointer on the screen, the mouse can also perform the following:

| Action | Result |
|---|---|
| Clicking | Clicking is simply pressing a mouse button. It may be the left or right button, both buttons simultaneously or the centre button if you have one. Normally you will have moved the mouse pointer to point at a menu option, or something similar, before clicking to select that option. |
| Double clicking | Double clicking involves pressing a mouse button twice very quickly. This is often used to both select and open a file in one go, for example within a word processor. Just how fast you need to double click can sometimes be changed from within the program itself. If you double click too slowly it will be treated as a two single clicks and may not have the desired effect. |
| Dragging | Dragging involves moving the mouse while holding down a mouse button. This technique is often used to mark a block of text. First you move the mouse pointer to the start of the block, then you drag the mouse over the text that is to form the block before releasing the button. |

## Mice problems

In this section you can read about the most common problems involving mice.

### A dirty mouse

Give the chance a mouse will travel several kilometre around your desk top. During this time it will inevitably pick up crumbs, hairs and other unwanted dust and dirt. If your mouse seems to start to stick, i.e. moving the mouse results in little or no movement of the mouse cursor, then the ball could be sticking and skidding across the table instead of rolling.

In this case it is just a matter of cleaning the mouse - usually a very simple operation.

Just turn the mouse upside down, unlock the cover keeping the ball in place and clean it. Then replace the cover.

### No mouse cursor

If there is no mouse cursor displayed then one of three things is happening - the mouse is not properly connected to your computer, the mouse driver has not been loaded, or the program you are using does not actually support a mouse or that it has been given the wrong information as to where to 'find' the mouse.

First check that the program supports a mouse. DOS, for example, will not itself display a mouse cursor. Then check the set-up procedures of that program to make sure that the mouse set-up is correctly selected, i.e. bus or serial mouse. You must also check to see if you have selected the correct serial port, i.e. serial port 1 or port 2.

Then check to see if the mouse driver has been installed. Look for a command in the CONFIG.SYS or AUTOEXEC.BAT file that includes a MOUSE.SYS or MOUSE.COM filename. If you do not find one then your computer is not made aware that a mouse is connected. Consult your mouse instruction book about installing the mouse software.

If neither of these help, then you will need to check the hardware to see if the mouse is properly connected. Retrace the steps in the instruction manual for your mouse. For a bus mouse check the IRQ selected does not collide with another accessory or use one of the many reserved IRQ lines. On the next page is a table showing the standard IRQ lines used:

| IRQ Line | IBM PC/XT | IBM AT/386 |
|---|---|---|
| 0 | System timer | System timer |
| 1 | Keyboard buffer | Keyboard buffer |
| 2 | Unused | Extended interrupt |
| 3 | Serial port 2 | Serial port 2 |
| 4 | Serial port 1 | Serial port 1 |
| 5 | Hard disk controller | Parallel port 2 |
| 6 | | Disk drive controller |
| 7 | Parallel port 1 | Parallel port 1 |
| 8 | | Real time clock |
| 13 | | Co-processor |
| 14 | | Hard disk controller |

## Other methods of data input

In this section you will find a brief description of some of the methods used to input data other than the keyboard and the mouse.

**Trackball**

A trackball is really a special sort of mouse with a ball on top rather than underneath. The ball can be rolled with the palm of your hand or with your fingertips. Choosing between a trackball and a mouse is a matter of preference

**Digitizing board**

Digitizing boards are commonly associated with CAD/CAM programs. In some ways they are similar to a mouse - moving the unit around on a special board rather than the desk top or mouse mat. However, digitizing boards often have a number of function pads which can be programmed to perform special functions.

**Light pen**

A light pen is not such a common input method, being mostly associated with CAD/CAM programs. By holding the pen against the screen its position is recorded and this information can be passed on to the program being used. By moving the pen around it is possible to draw different figures. Connection requires a special connector on a multi-function card.

**Joystick**

A joystick is associated with games. It is a lever type unit that can be moved in all directions and has a "fire" button. A joystick must be connected to a games port. Some computers have a games port when delivered, some serial port expansion cards will also have a games port.

**Scanner**

A scanner is a special machine for reading in a picture. The scanner itself can be a full A4 page reader or a small hand-held unit that is moved around a page. Most scanners work in black and white and can produce different grey scales. Colour scanners are, however, fast appearing on the market. The result of a scanned page is always a picture - even if you scan in a text. A special so-called OCR program can convert scanned texts from a picture to actual text that can then be used in your word processor.

# 8. Danger: Computer Virus at Large

Most computer users these days will have heard about PC viruses. Friday 13th has become more than a day for superstitions, it has become a day of worry for many users. Newspaper headlines and news broadcasts across the industrial world have spread fear amongst new and experienced computer people. The threat that computer viruses pose is becoming a regular topic in computer magazines.

In this chapter, you can learn about computer viruses, judge if you are at risk yourself, and find out what to do if your computer is affected. A survey of some of the most common viruses will help you to recognise some of the symptoms.

## What is a virus?

Basically a computer virus is a small computer program that manages to copy itself onto your computer - onto a floppy or hard disk. Think of them as weeds in your vegetable patch - they turn up without asking, and if you don't pull them out they will gradually take over the entire patch.

Some weeds are in fact quite attractive, but most of them are simply a nuisance. The same is true of computer viruses, a few are light-hearted or even humorous, the majority are, however, designed to damage the data you have stored on floppy or hard disks. That is why they are dangerous. In the worst-case scenario your computer could have a complete breakdown and you could loose all the information stored on your hard disk and on one or more of your floppy disks. If you don't want Fu Manchu or the Dark Avenger striking you down with a digital potato blight, then read on!

Here is a brief summary of some of the terms used in connection with computer viruses:

**Virus:** A small program that can copy itself "into" other programs. Viruses affect other existing programs and are dependent on them as they do not exist as complete programs themselves.

**Time bomb:** A small program section (normally destructive) that is activated when certain predefined conditions are met, e.g. a specific date and/or time, a specified period after the being installed, a predefined keyboard sequence or a specified number of times a program is run.

**Trojan horse:** This is a program which will perform a specific normal task, just as any other program does, but also contains a hidden and undesirable part.

**Bacteria or worms:** Stand-alone programs, unlike viruses which 'attach' themselves to other programs, that create copies of themselves on the same computer and on other computers, thus decreasing available memory and 'choking' the computer..

## Am I at risk?

Yes.

If you own a computer, or are responsible for one, for example at work, then you are at risk. If a virus strikes, then you may lose some vital information, and loose time by having to deal with the situation.

If you are an occasional user using somebody else's computer, then the risk is limited to the effect that you may loose some of your important work, apart from the possible embarrassment of having to tell the owner that his computer really ought to see a doctor.

If you are a nervous or reserved computer beginner, then you may well suffer psychologically as you realise that you have to face up to a very awkward situation with a total lack of confidence. Read on!

## Catching viruses

"Catching viruses" should perhaps be re-phrased as "Getting caught by viruses" as no-one actually goes out looking for the things. The strange thing is that some users tend to be hypersensitive and a mere hiccough from their computer is construed as a true sign of a virus closing in for the kill, and "..wait till I get my hands on...?". Yes, who is the guilty one?

Seriously, many hitches, system hang-ups, computers going down, etc., depend on things other than viruses. Wrongly given commands, programs that do not work properly, variations in the power supply and memory resident programs can all cause problems that can be misconstrued as a virus.

Viruses move from one computer to another via floppy disks and communications. If you are given a floppy disk it could contain a virus that automatically copies itself onto your hard disk when you use the diskette. Having an infested diskette or hard disk could mean that the virus copies itself onto each diskette that you use, and can possibly be passed on to someone else. Thus viruses have a nasty habit of spreading, without anyone knowing anything about it.

If you buy a new computer and buy new programs which you use to create your own data, then you will "clean".

If you accept a diskette from a friend or work mate, and use that diskette in your computer, then you put yourself at risk, although each time you do so the risk is very very small.

If you connect your computer to others, in a network or with the help of a communications program, then you also put yourself at risk. Again each time you do so the risk is very very small. BBS (Bulletin Board

Systems) that have untested programs on offer are well-known virus transmitters.

## .COM and .EXE files are hit

A virus works by "adding" its own program code to an existing program file - .COM or .EXE file, data files are not affected. For example your word processor that was 92 200 bytes in size could suddenly grow to 92 965 bytes in size - a true sign that it has been hit by a virus program.

Some viruses will affect important system files such as the COMMAND.COM file. Another type of virus affects the boot sector of diskettes, which is where vital information about the contents of the diskette is held.

## Where do viruses come from?

Viruses are small computer programs. They are constructed by able programmers with a lot of time on their hands. Writing an effective virus program that doesn't give itself away is a time consuming process.

Some people see viruses as some sort of mischievous sport, good for a laugh. However, you cannot hide the fact that viruses constitute sabotage, a desire to inflict damage to other peoples' computers, programs and data.

Viruses have been traced from USA, UK, West Germany, Israel, Iceland, Bulgaria, India, Pakistan and many other countries.

## Some examples

At the time of writing there are over 150 known virus programs, and that figure is rising all the time. Old viruses are improved, variations appear and new devilments are created.

Here is a summary of just a few of the most widely spread viruses. Remember that some viruses have several names, and some are more harmful than others.

## Alabama

Other names or variants: Not known.

Recognition: .EXE files grow by 1560 bytes.

Effects: When the hour changes on your computer's clock the message "SOFTWARE COPIES ARE PROHIBITED BY INTERNATIONAL LAW" and the address "Box 1055, Tuscambia, ALABAMA" is displayed. The computer will then hang (i.e. stop working). Alabama can even survive a **Ctrl + Alt + Del** reboot.

## Brain

Other names or variants: Ashar, Lahore, Pakistani

Recognition: Affects diskettes, you will see the volume label as (C) Brain

Effects: An infected computer will transmit this virus to each new diskette you use. No other significant effects.

## Cascade

Other names or variants: 1701, 1704, Second Austrian, Blackjack, Autumn, Waterfall, Falling Letters

Recognition: .COM files grow by 1701 bytes (some versions 1704 bytes).

Effects: When activated, characters displayed on your screen fall into a pile at the bottom of the screen giving a click sound for each letter that falls.

## Dark Avenger

Other names or variants: Eddie 2

Recognition: .COM and .EXE files grow by 1800 bytes.

Effects: Writes a string starting "Eddie lives..." at random places on a hard disk and at random intervals.

## Dbase

Other names or variants: Not known

Recognition: .COM files grow by 1864 bytes. A hidden file BUGS.DAT in the root directory is also created.

Effects: All files with the extension .DBF are changed.

## Datacrime

Other names or variants: 1168, Datacrime II

Recognition: .COM files grow by 1168 bytes (some versions by 1280 bytes).

Effects: On October 13th each year, and every day thereafter until December 31st it displays the message "DATACRIME VIRUS RELEASED 1 MARCH 1989". Then it starts formatting a vital part of your hard disk (FAT, File Allocation Table), which means that your computer will not be able to find files any longer.

## Denzuk

Other names or variants: Venezulan, Search, Denzuk 1

Recognition: If you have a colour monitor and reboot your computer using **Ctrl+Alt+Del**, the word "Denzuk" is displayed together with the Denzuk logotype. Pressing **Ctrl+Alt+F5** may also give the same result. The Volume label may also be changed to Y.C.I.E.R.P

Effects: Denzuk also looks for Brain and will remove brain and install itself. Denzuk also assumes that all diskettes are 360 kb and may cause other problems with other types of diskette.

## Fumble

Other names or variants: Not known.

Effects: Exchanges keys pressed with the key immediately to the right on the keyboard. It is activated by fast typists, i.e. more than 60 characters per minute. No damage to disks is done.

## Fu Manchu

Other names or variants: 2086.

Recognition: .COM files grow by 2086 bytes, and .EXE files by a similar amount. If you reboot your computer using **Ctrl+Alt+Del** the sentence "`The world will hear from me again!`" is displayed.

Effects: If you type Thatcher, Reagan, Waldheim or Botha it adds "`is a ????`", where ???? is a well-known four letter word. Also, if you type a four letter swear word, it will erase that word. If you type "`Fu Manchu`" it will confirm its existence with "`Fu Manchu virus 3/10/88 - latest in the new line of fun`".

## Italian

Other names or variants: Ping pong, Bouncing ball.

Recognition: Disks will have a bad cluster, 512 bytes, 1 or 2 kb. Once every 30 minutes, if you are accessing a disk, a bouncing dot is displayed.

Effects: Does not affect 286 or 386 machines.

## Jerusalem

Other names or variants: 1813, Israeli, PLO, Friday 13th.

Recognition: .COM files grow once by 1813 bytes. .EXE files grow indefinite by about 1808 bytes until they become too large to run.

Effects: Every Friday 13th any program you run is deleted. 30 minutes after running an infected program (on any date), the computer will appear to slow down.

## June 16th

Other names or variants: Not known.

Recognition: .COM files grow by 879 bytes.

Effects: Every June 16th, it scans the current drive directory and renames any file it finds to "ZAPPED".

## Ogre

Other names or variants: Computer Ogre, Disk Killer

Recognition: 8 kb memory is lost. Diskettes have 3 kb of bad sectors.

Effects: If you leave your computer on for 48 hours and then within the next hour access a hard disk, then the following message is displayed "`Disk Killer version 1.0`", and you are warned not to turn off your computer. Your hard disk will then be encrypted, and thus rendered unusable.

## Stoned

Other names or variants: New Zealand, Marijuana.

Recognition: Every eighth time you start your computer, the message "`Your computer is now stoned`" is displayed.

Effects: Infects all diskettes you use. Can cause problems with 1.2 Mb diskettes and 3.5" diskettes, by overwriting some directory entries.

## Ten bytes

Other names or variants: 1554

Recognition: .COM files grow by between 1554 and 1569 bytes.

Effects: Every year from September to December, when writing files to a disk, the first 10 characters are omitted and 10 garbage characters are added to the end of the file instead.

## Typo

Other names or variants: Not known.

Effects: Changes some characters sent to a printer port, e.g. changes V to W.

## Vienna

Other names or variants: 648, 1 in 8, Austrian, DOS 62, Lisbon.

Recognition: .COM files grow by 648 bytes.

Effects: Destroys each eighth file. Eventually COMMAND.COM is infected, and whenever the computer is started up it keeps rebooting or just hangs.

### Yankee Doodle

Other names or variants: Vascina and many others.

Recognition: .COM files grow between 2771 and 2900 bytes. .EXE files also grow.

Effects: At 5.00 pm the virus plays Yankee Doodle Dandee.

### Zerobug

Other names or variants: Zero Eater

Recognition: .COM files grow by 1536 bytes.

Effects: A face works its way down the screen "eating" all the zeros.

### 765

Other names or variants: Perfume

Recognition: .COM files grow by 765 bytes.

Effects: After an infected file has been run 80 times, a message is displayed. If you type "`4711`" the program will continue to run, any other entry will cause the program to terminate.

## Recognising viruses

Many computer users mistakenly think that they have been hit by a virus. If you have read about the example viruses, you will have some idea as to the kind of thing that can happen. If something strange happens to your computer you really need to keep your head and try and think "Have I done something wrong here?". The picture is complicated by the fact that there are bugs (mistakes) in some programs on sale that could cause odd things to happen. However, these are usually limited to a certain function of a program not working properly, or that the computer simply hangs.

Dr. Alan Solomon, perhaps the world's leading computer virus expert, has been quoted as saying that he believes that one or two percent of computer have been affected. If his estimation is correct then if something crazy happens on your computer there is a small chance that you have a virus, but it is probable that you do not.

For example, if sometimes when starting your computer it hangs, i.e. locks itself, several times before getting going, then this may be a particular hardware failure. If on the other hand it does so and at the same time gives off five beeps every now and again, then you should begin to ask yourself if it is a virus at large.

It can be very difficult trying to trace a virus. Fumble, as described earlier, will hit anyone typing at faster speeds, i.e. a secretary. Calling in a techie to try and fix the bug will probably not reveal anything because he/she types to slowly to activate the virus. Some viruses are inspired mischievous sabotage!

If you have an original program diskette that you bought, check the size of the .COM and .EXE program files on the original diskette against the file sizes on your hard disk (be sure that the original diskettes are write-protected before doing so!). If any of the files have grown, then you should suspect a virus.

If you suspect that your computer has been infected, you will need to remove all the infected files. An anti-virus program (see last section in this chapter) can also be of great help.

## Preventative measures

There are some measures that you can take to protect yourself against viruses. A single PC is easier to protect than a system of computers connected together in a network.

One major point is never to accept a diskette from anyone without knowing where it came from. Your best friend could easily and unknowingly pass on an infected diskette to you. As soon as you use that diskette a virus could be transferred to your computer.

Always write-protect your original program diskettes before installing programs on your computer. Write-protection works as a virus preventative too. Write-protect other important diskettes that are not going to be written to.

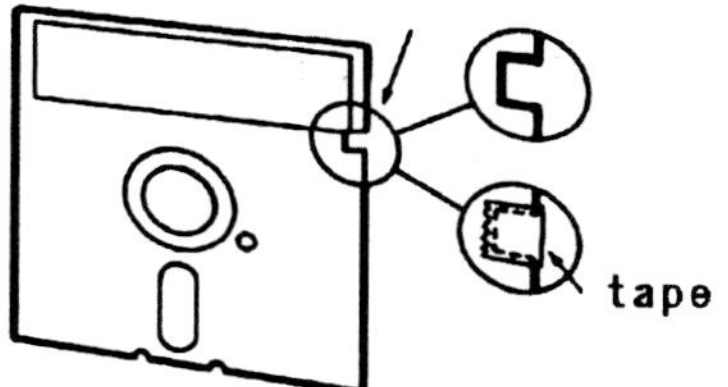


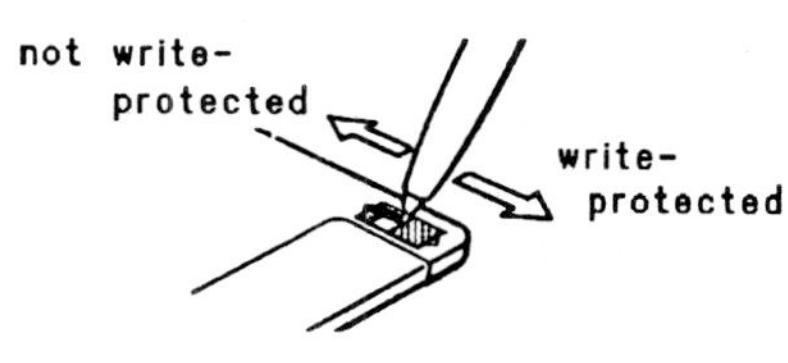


As viruses often affect the important system file called COMMAND.COM, you should make a copy of this file on your hard disk or system diskette. Then compare the original COMMAND.COM file with the copy each time you start your computer. There is a special DOS command for doing this and you can put it in your AUTOEXEC.BAT file. When you start your computer you will then be notified if the two files are not the same, i.e. the COMMAND.COM file has mysteriously been changed. The steps are as follows:

- First start your computer and wait for the prompt `A:>` or `C:>`.
- Type:

```
copy command.com cmmnd.cm
```

Now add the following command to your AUTOEXEC.BAT file:

**fc command.com cmmnd.cm**

---

*Note:*
*Some DOS versions use* **comp** *instead of* **fc**.

---

## Anti-virus programs - prevention or cure?

Several programs that reveal the presence of viruses can be found on the market. They cannot help when a virus has already struck and your hard disk has been erased, but they can help you by warning you when a virus installs itself and in some cases even remove the virus or prevent it installing itself.

The easiest way to test for viruses is by checking the size of program files - as you have already read many viruses attach themselves to other files which grow by a corresponding amount. Many anti-virus programs work this way. The problem here is that they can only protect uninfected systems - if you already have a virus it's too late. This type of program will not detect other virus types that tamper with system files and information such as changing track 0 of your hard disk.

Another type of protection is to have a memory resident program to check for viruses. If a virus tries to increase its size or go memory resident itself, then this must take up some of the resources available. These resources can be monitored.

One program that deserves a special mention is **Dr. Solomon's Toolkit**, which is a combination of several programs designed to combat viruses. This has been programmed to recognize a large number of viruses and updates are released at regular intervals. Apart from finding most known viruses, it can inoculate your computer against some viruses thus preventing these viruses installing themselves. The handbook is also very well written and describes in more detail how viruses work and explains most known viruses.

# Summary

- Computer viruses are small and dangerous programs that can very quickly spread and grow.
- Many viruses attach themselves to other programs, thus increasing the size of the program file.
- Some viruses plant themselves on the boot sector of a disk, which the computer needs to read when you start it.
- Other viruses can hide on other parts of a disk which become marked as 'bad sectors'.
- Viruses are spread in general by diskettes - check what you are getting.
- Another common method of picking up a virus is communications, especially BBS systems with plenty of free programs to be downloaded.
- Write-protection will protect your diskettes from viruses.
- Anti-virus programs can help you detect viruses.

# A. The ASCII and PostScript Character Sets

Your computer is not only capable of producing letters and numbers, it can also produce many graphic characters. These characters can be used with certain programs, for example, to create boxes and lines.

To write these characters, which are not displayed on any of the keys on your keyboard, you need to press the **Alt** key, in conjunction with a number code, using the number keys on the right-hand side of the keyboard.

A table of available characters is displayed below. To obtain a character in the table, you must look up its number code. The example below will type an Ä character.

- Hold down the **Alt** key.
- Type in the code number for the desired character, using the number key pad on the right-hand side of the keyboard, for example:

  `142`

- Release the **Alt** key.

This will not necessarily work for all programs or printers, since some use their own character sets. In such cases, you should consult the appropriate manual.

Furthermore the ASCII and PostScript character sets, and other character sets, differ. Choosing a number code will sometimes select different characters depending on what character set is being used by the program - this is particularly relevant to desktop publishing. On a few occasions, different characters will be printed to those displayed on your screen! Your printer might not have the same character set as that used on the screen - only code numbers are sent to the printer not a simple copy of what is displayed. The following tables display some of the character sets.

# The ASCII character set

This character set is the standard character set.

| 21 = | § | 69 = | E | 107 = | k | 145 = | æ | 183 = | ╖ | 221 = | ▌ |
|---|---|---|---|---|---|---|---|---|---|---|---|
| 32 = |  | 70 = | F | 108 = | l | 146 = | Æ | 184 = | ╕ | 222 = | ▐ |
| 33 = | ! | 71 = | G | 109 = | m | 147 = | ô | 185 = | ╣ | 223 = | ▀ |
| 34 = | " | 72 = | H | 110 = | n | 148 = | ö | 186 = | ║ | 224 = | α |
| 35 = | # | 73 = | I | 111 = | o | 149 = | ò | 187 = | ╗ | 225 = | β |
| 36 = | % | 74 = | J | 112 = | p | 150 = | û | 188 = | ╝ | 226 = | Γ |
| 37 = |  | 75 = | K | 113 = | q | 151 = | ù | 189 = | ╜ | 227 = | π |
| 38 = | & | 76 = | L | 114 = | r | 152 = | ÿ | 190 = | ╛ | 228 = | Σ |
| 39 = | ' | 77 = | M | 115 = | s | 153 = | Ö | 191 = | ┐ | 229 = | σ |
| 40 = | ( | 78 = | N | 116 = | t | 154 = | Ü | 192 = | └ | 230 = | µ |
| 41 = | ) | 79 = | O | 117 = | u | 155 = | ¢ | 193 = | ┴ | 231 = | τ |
| 42 = | * | 80 = | P | 118 = | v | 156 = |  | 194 = | ┬ | 232 = | Φ |
| 43 = | + | 81 = | Q | 119 = | w | 157 = | ¥ | 195 = | ├ | 233 = | Θ |
| 44 = | , | 82 = | R | 120 = | x | 158 = | ₧ | 196 = | ─ | 234 = | Ω |
| 45 = | – | 83 = | S | 121 = | y | 159 = | ƒ | 197 = | ┼ | 235 = | δ |
| 46 = | . | 84 = | T | 122 = | z | 160 = | á | 198 = | ╞ | 236 = | ∞ |
| 47 = | / | 85 = | U | 123 = | { | 161 = | í | 199 = | ╟ | 237 = | φ |
| 48 = | 0 | 86 = | V | 124 = | ¦ | 162 = | ó | 200 = | ╚ | 238 = | ε |
| 49 = | 1 | 87 = | W | 125 = | } | 163 = | ú | 201 = | ╔ | 239 = | ∩ |
| 50 = | 2 | 88 = | X | 126 = | ~ | 164 = | ñ | 202 = | ╩ | 240 = | ≡ |
| 51 = | 3 | 89 = | Y | 127 = | ⌂ | 165 = | Ñ | 203 = | ╦ | 241 = | ± |
| 52 = | 4 | 90 = | Z | 128 = | Ç | 166 = | ª | 204 = | ╠ | 242 = | ≥ |
| 53 = | 5 | 91 = | [ | 129 = | ü | 167 = | º | 205 = | ═ | 243 = | ≤ |
| 54 = | 6 | 92 = | \ | 130 = | é | 168 = | ¿ | 206 = | ╬ | 244 = | ⌠ |
| 55 = | 7 | 93 = | ] | 131 = | â | 169 = | ⌐ | 207 = | ╧ | 245 = | ⌡ |
| 56 = | 8 | 94 = | ^ | 132 = | ä | 170 = | ¬ | 208 = | ╨ | 246 = | ÷ |
| 57 = | 9 | 95 = | _ | 133 = | à | 171 = | ½ | 209 = | ╤ | 247 = | ≈ |
| 58 = | : | 96 = | ` | 134 = | å | 172 = | ¼ | 210 = | ╥ | 248 = | ° |
| 59 = | ; | 97 = | a | 135 = | ç | 173 = | ¡ | 211 = | ╙ | 249 = | ● |
| 60 = | < | 98 = | b | 136 = | ê | 174 = | « | 212 = | ╘ | 250 = | · |
| 61 = | = | 99 = | c | 137 = | ë | 175 = | » | 213 = | ╒ | 251 = | √ |
| 62 = | > | 100 = | d | 138 = | è | 176 = | ░ | 214 = | ╓ | 252 = | ⁿ |
| 63 = | ? | 101 = | e | 139 = | ï | 177 = | ▒ | 215 = | ╫ | 253 = | ² |
| 64 = | @ | 102 = | f | 140 = | î | 178 = | ▓ | 216 = | ╪ | 254 = | ■ |
| 65 = | A | 103 = | g | 141 = | ì | 179 = | │ | 217 = | ┘ | 255 = |  |
| 66 = | B | 104 = | h | 142 = | Ä | 180 = | ┤ | 218 = | ┌ |  |  |
| 67 = | C | 105 = | i | 143 = | Å | 181 = | ╡ | 219 = | █ |  |  |
| 68 = | D | 106 = | j | 144 = | É | 182 = | ╢ | 220 = | ▄ |  |  |

# Other character sets

The International, Symbol and Dingbat character sets, shown in the following table, are commonly used in desktop publishing and PostScript printers.

| Decimal | Internat'l | Symbol | Dingbat | Decimal | Internat'l | Symbol | Dingbat | Decimal | Internat'l | Symbol | Dingbat | Decimal | Internat'l | Symbol | Dingbat | Decimal | Internat'l | Symbol | Dingbat |
|---|---|---|---|---|---|---|---|---|---|---|---|---|---|---|---|---|---|---|---|
| 32 | | | | 53 | 5 | 5 | ✕ | 74 | J | ϑ | ✪ | 95 | _ | _ | ✿ | 116 | t | τ | ▼ |
| 33 | ! | ! | ✁ | 54 | 6 | 6 | ✖ | 75 | K | Κ | ✫ | 96 | ' | ‾ | ❀ | 117 | u | υ | ◆ |
| 34 | " | ∀ | ✂ | 55 | 7 | 7 | ✗ | 76 | L | Λ | ✬ | 97 | a | α | ❁ | 118 | v | ϖ | ❖ |
| 35 | # | # | ✃ | 56 | 8 | 8 | ✘ | 77 | M | Μ | ✭ | 98 | b | β | ❂ | 119 | w | ω | ◗ |
| 36 | $ | ∃ | ✄ | 57 | 9 | 9 | ✙ | 78 | N | Ν | ✮ | 99 | c | χ | ❃ | 120 | x | ξ | ❘ |
| 37 | % | % | ☎ | 58 | : | : | ✚ | 79 | O | Ο | ✯ | 100 | d | δ | ❄ | 121 | y | ψ | ❙ |
| 38 | & | & | ✆ | 59 | ; | ; | ✛ | 80 | P | Π | ✰ | 101 | e | ε | ❅ | 122 | z | ζ | ❚ |
| 39 | ' | ∋ | ✇ | 60 | < | < | ✜ | 81 | Q | Θ | ✱ | 102 | f | φ | ❆ | 123 | { | { | ❛ |
| 40 | ( | ( | ✈ | 61 | = | = | ✝ | 82 | R | Ρ | ✲ | 103 | g | γ | ❇ | 124 | \| | \| | ❜ |
| 41 | ) | ) | ✉ | 62 | > | > | ✞ | 83 | S | Σ | ✳ | 104 | h | η | ❈ | 125 | } | } | ❝ |
| 42 | * | ∗ | ☛ | 63 | ? | ? | ✟ | 84 | T | Τ | ✴ | 105 | i | ι | ❉ | 126 | ~ | ~ | ❞ |
| 43 | + | + | ☞ | 64 | @ | ≅ | ✠ | 85 | U | Υ | ✵ | 106 | j | ϕ | ❊ | 127 | | | |
| 44 | , | , | ✌ | 65 | A | Α | ✡ | 86 | V | ς | ✶ | 107 | k | κ | ❋ | 128 | Ç | | |
| 45 | - | − | ✍ | 66 | B | Β | ✢ | 87 | W | Ω | ✷ | 108 | l | λ | ● | 129 | ü | ϒ | ❡ |
| 46 | . | . | ✎ | 67 | C | Χ | ✣ | 88 | X | Ξ | ✸ | 109 | m | μ | ❍ | 130 | é | ′ | ❢ |
| 47 | / | / | ✏ | 68 | D | Δ | ✤ | 89 | Y | Ψ | ✹ | 110 | n | ν | ■ | 131 | â | ≤ | ❣ |
| 48 | 0 | 0 | ✐ | 69 | E | Ε | ✥ | 90 | Z | Ζ | ✺ | 111 | o | ο | ❏ | 132 | ä | ⁄ | ❤ |
| 49 | 1 | 1 | ✑ | 70 | F | Φ | ✦ | 91 | [ | [ | ✻ | 112 | p | π | ❐ | 133 | à | ∞ | ❥ |
| 50 | 2 | 2 | ✒ | 71 | G | Γ | ✧ | 92 | \ | ∴ | ✼ | 113 | q | θ | ❑ | 134 | å | ƒ | ❦ |
| 51 | 3 | 3 | ✓ | 72 | H | Η | ★ | 93 | ] | ] | ✽ | 114 | r | ρ | ❒ | 135 | ç | ♣ | ❧ |
| 52 | 4 | 4 | ✔ | 73 | I | Ι | ✩ | 94 | ^ | ⊥ | ✾ | 115 | s | σ | ▲ | 136 | ê | ♦ | ♣ |

| Decimal | Internat'l | Symbol | Dingbat | Decimal | Internat'l | Symbol | Dingbat | Decimal | Internat'l | Symbol | Dingbat | Decimal | Internat'l | Symbol | Dingbat |
|---|---|---|---|---|---|---|---|---|---|---|---|---|---|---|---|
| 137 | ë | ♥ | ♦ | 158 | ¤ | — | ❾ | 179 | ø | © | ➓ | 200 | Â | ⎝ | ➨ |
| 138 | è | ♠ | ♥ | 159 | ƒ | ↵ | ❿ | 180 | œ | ™ | ➔ | 201 | È | ⎡ | ➩ |
| 139 | ï | ↔ | ♠ | 160 | á | ℵ | ① | 181 | Œ | Π | → | 202 | Ê | ⎢ | ➪ |
| 140 | î | ← | ① | 161 | í | ℑ | ② | 182 | À | √ | ↔ | 203 | Ë | ⎣ | ➫ |
| 141 | ì | ↑ | ② | 162 | ó | ℜ | ③ | 183 | Ã | · | ↕ | 204 | Ì | ⎧ | ➬ |
| 142 | Ä | → | ③ | 163 | ú | ℘ | ④ | 184 | Õ | ¬ | ➘ | 205 | Í | ⎨ | ➭ |
| 143 | Å | ↓ | ④ | 164 | ñ | ⊗ | ⑤ | 185 | § | ∧ | ➙ | 206 | Î | ⎩ | ➮ |
| 144 | É | ° | ⑤ | 165 | Ñ | ⊕ | ⑥ | 186 | ‡ | ∨ | ➚ | 207 | Ï | ⎪ | ➯ |
| 145 | æ | ± | ⑥ | 166 | ª | ∅ | ⑦ | 187 | † | ⇔ | ➛ | 208 | Ò | | |
| 146 | Æ | ″ | ⑦ | 167 | º | ∩ | ⑧ | 188 | ¶ | ⇐ | ➜ | 209 | Ó | 〉 | ➱ |
| 147 | ô | ≥ | ⑧ | 168 | ¿ | ∪ | ⑨ | 189 | © | ⇑ | ➝ | 210 | Ô | ∫ | ➲ |
| 148 | ö | × | ⑨ | 169 | “ | ⊃ | ⑩ | 190 | ® | ⇒ | ➞ | 211 | Š | ⌠ | ➳ |
| 149 | ò | ∝ | ⑩ | 170 | ” | ⊇ | ➊ | 191 | ™ | ⇓ | ➟ | 212 | š | ⎮ | ➴ |
| 150 | û | ∂ | ❶ | 171 | ‹ | ⊄ | ➋ | 192 | „ | ◊ | ➠ | 213 | Ù | ⌡ | ➵ |
| 151 | ù | • | ❷ | 172 | › | ⊂ | ➌ | 193 | … | 〈 | ➡ | 214 | Ú | ⎞ | ➶ |
| 152 | ÿ | ÷ | ❸ | 173 | ¡ | ⊆ | ➍ | 194 | ‰ | ® | ➢ | 215 | Û | ⎟ | ➷ |
| 153 | Ö | ≠ | ❹ | 174 | « | ∈ | ➎ | 195 | • | © | ➣ | 216 | Ÿ | ⎠ | ➸ |
| 154 | Ü | ≡ | ❺ | 175 | » | ∉ | ➏ | 196 | – | ™ | ➤ | 217 | ß | ⎤ | ➹ |
| 155 | ¢ | ≈ | ❻ | 176 | ã | ∠ | ➐ | 197 | — | Σ | ➥ | 218 | Ž | ⎥ | ➺ |
| 156 | £ | … | ❼ | 177 | õ | ∇ | ➑ | 198 | ° | ⎛ | ➦ | | | | |
| 157 | ¥ | \| | ❽ | 178 | Ø | ® | ➒ | 199 | Á | ⎜ | ➧ | | | | |

# B: Example Batch Files for Formatting Diskettes

In this appendix you will find instructions about how to create your own batch file that will simplify the formatting process. Because it is assumed that you have read through the previous chapter on batch files, the batch commands used will not be re-explained here.

Several different batch files are presented. The first three show examples of how to set up batch files specifically designed for your system. The fourth example looks at how to solve the formatting problem by allowing for all possible combinations, but does require that the user knows just what type of drive is to be used and what type of diskette he/she wants to format.

How much explanatory information you bake into the batch file should also depend on the eventual user(s) of the program. If you are setting up a batch file for yourself only, you will probably need the minimal of text. If you are setting up the file for a friend or work mate, he/she may benefit from more explanations. It is also very quick and easy to change the batch file at any time if necessary.

## Preparations

The FORMAT command is an external DOS command and must therefore be available when you want to format a diskette. If you have a hard disk then this should present no problems, you can simply create the batch file in the same subdirectory as the standard FORMAT command. For diskette based systems, when formatting a diskette you need to use your DOS diskette, so the obvious thing to do is to create any batch file directly on the DOS diskette. In both cases follow the instructions below each time you create a batch file for formatting.

### Diskette based systems

To create any of the following example batch files on your DOS diskette first do as follows:

- Insert your DOS diskette in drive A.

You must also make sure that A is the active drive as follows:

- Type:

  ```
  a:
  ```

- Press the ↵ key.

### Hard disk systems

To create any of the following example batch files in your DOS subdirectory, first do as follows:

- Type:

  ```
  c:
  ```

- Press the ↵ key.
- Type:

  ```
  cd \dos
  ```

- Press the ↵ key.

## Examples

The examples give a listing of the completed file only. As explained in the previous chapter, there are three ways of creating a batch file, using the command COPY CON, using EDLIN or using your own word processor/editor program. Choose whichever method you feel most comfortable with.

The method used is quite simple. The program is called FMT.BAT and expects a variable to be given, for example, FMT 1 or FMT 2. When no variable is given, and just the filename FMT, then a help page is displayed instead, giving you instructions on what variable to use.

DOS checks the variable given, and moves to the right label in the batch file to perform the format. After formatting, several formats of the same type are allowed, the program jumps to the stop label and is concluded.

## Example 1

Example 1 assumes that you have a system with two standard 5.25" 360 kb drives. The B drive is always used to format a diskette, as with a diskette based system the DOS diskette can be inserted in drive A and the diskette to be formatted in drive B. For a hard disk system this does not apply.

Here is the file in full:

```
echo off
if "%1" = = "1" goto form1
if "%1" = = "2" goto form2
goto help
:help
cls
echo *
echo *   FORMATTING SERVICE  -  Peter's PC
echo *
= = = = = = = = = = = = = = = = = = = = = = = = = = = = = = = = =
echo *
echo *   The only type of diskettes you can format are standard
echo *   360 kb 5.25" diskettes.
echo *
echo *   You can however choose to format a system diskette or not.
echo *
echo *   Type FMT 1 to format a non-system diskette in drive B
echo *   Type FMT 2 to format a system diskette in drive B
goto stop
:form1
cls
echo *
echo *   FORMATTING SERVICE
echo *   = = = = = = = = = = = = = = = = = =
echo *
echo *   Format a standard non-system diskette in drive B.
echo *   Cancel with Ctrl + C or
echo *
pause
format b:
goto stop
:form2
cls
echo *
echo *   FORMATTING SERVICE
echo *   = = = = = = = = = = = = = = = = = =
echo *
echo *   Format a standard SYSTEM diskette in drive B.
echo *   Cancel with Ctrl + C or
echo *
pause
format b:/s
goto stop
```

```
:stop
echo  *
echo  *
echo  *    End of formatting service.
echo  *
```

As you can see, a lot of effort is put into making the program readable and easy to understand for the user. A shortened version with only the necessary program lines would look like this:

```
cls
if "%1" = = "1" goto form1
if "%1" = = "2" goto form2
echo  *    Type FMT 1 to format a non-system diskette in drive B
echo  *    Type FMT 2 to format a system diskette in drive B
goto stop
:form1
format b:
goto stop
:form2
format b:/s
goto stop
:stop
```

The version that you would use would probably depend on the user's knowledge.

- To try the program, type in one of the versions and call the file FMT.BAT.
- To run the program type:

  `fmt`
- Press the ↵ key.

Lines 2 & 3 (of both versions) check to see if a matching variable has been given with the command, and if so sends the program to the correct subroutine or label.

```
if "%1" = = "1" goto form1
if "%1" = = "2" goto form2
```

If no matching variable is found, then the program proceeds to the help subroutine, displays the help page and then proceeds to the stop label, where the program ends. You can then type in a new FMT command.

## Example 2

This example program is suited to a system with a single 5.25" high-density drive. It is possible to format 360 kb and 1.2 Mb diskettes, and make them system diskettes or not. The program is written using the same method as example 1. First a section to catch a variable on the command line, then a help page, and finally the separate subroutines to initiate the actual FORMAT command.

```
echo off
if "%1" = = "1" goto form1
if "%1" = = "2" goto form2
if "%1" = = "3" goto form3
if "%1" = = "4" goto form4
goto help
:help
cls
echo *
echo *   FORMATTING SERVICE - Peter's XT
echo *
= = = = = = = = = = = = = = = = = = = = = = = = = = = = = = = = =
echo *
echo *   You can choose to format a standard diskette (360 kb)
echo *   or a high-density diskette (HD 1.2 Mb).
echo *
echo *   You can also choose to make it a system diskette or not.
echo *
echo *   Type FMT 1 to format a standard 360 kb non-system diskette
echo *   Type FMT 2 to format a standard 360 kb system diskette
echo *   Type FMT 3 to format a HD 1.2 Mb non-system diskette
echo *   Type FMT 4 to format a HD 1.2 Mb system diskette
goto stop
:form1
cls
echo *
echo *   FORMATTING SERVICE
echo *   = = = = = = = = = = = = = = = = = = =
echo *
echo *   Format a standard non-system diskette 360 kb
echo *   Cancel with Ctrl + C or
echo *
pause
format a:/4
goto stop
:form2
cls
echo *
echo *   FORMATTING SERVICE
echo *   = = = = = = = = = = = = = = = = = = =
echo *
echo *   Format a standard SYSTEM diskette 360 kb.
echo *   Cancel with Ctrl + C or
echo *
pause
```

```
format a:/4/s
goto stop
:form3
cls
echo *
echo *   FORMATTING SERVICE
echo *   ====================
echo *
echo *   Format a HD non-system diskette 1.2 MB
echo *   Cancel with Ctrl+C or
echo *
pause
format a:
goto stop
:form4
cls
echo *
echo *   FORMATTING SERVICE
echo *   ====================
echo *
echo *   Format a HD SYSTEM diskette 1.2 Mb
echo *   Cancel with Ctrl+C or
echo *
pause
format a:/s
goto stop
:stop
echo *
echo *
echo *   End of formatting service.
echo *
```

Without all the explanations, this program could be reduced to just 25 lines.

## Example 3

By copying example 2 and just changing a few of the text lines and the four lines with the actual FORMAT command on, you could easily produce the following example. It is devised for a system with a high-density 5.25" drive as drive A, and a high-density 3.5" drive as drive B.

```
echo off

if "%1" == "1" goto form1
if "%1" == "2" goto form2
if "%1" == "3" goto form3
if "%1" == "4" goto form4
goto help
:help
cls
echo *
```

```
echo *   FORMATTING SERVICE  -  Peter's AT
echo *
===================================
echo *
echo *   Type one of the following commands:
echo *
echo *   Command     Diskette format
echo *   --------------------------
echo *   FMT 1       5.25"  360 kb
echo *   FMT 2       5.25"  1.2 Mb  (HD)
echo *
echo *   FMT 3       3.5"  720 kb
echo *   FMT 4       3.5"  1.44 Mb  (HD)
goto stop
:form1
cls
echo *
echo *   FORMATTING SERVICE
echo *   ===================
echo *
echo *   Format a standard 5.25" 360 kb diskette in drive A
echo *   Cancel with Ctrl + C or
echo *
pause
format a:/4
goto stop
:form2
cls
echo *
echo *   FORMATTING SERVICE
echo *   ===================
echo *
echo *   Format a HD 5.25" 1.2 Mb diskette in drive A
echo *   Cancel with Ctrl + C or
echo *
pause
format a:
goto stop
:form3
cls
echo *
echo *   FORMATTING SERVICE
echo *   ===================
echo *
echo *   Format a standard 3.5" 720 kb diskette in drive B
echo *   Cancel with Ctrl + C or
echo *
pause
format b:/f:720
goto stop
:form4
cls
echo *
echo *   FORMATTING SERVICE
echo *   ===================
echo *
```

```
echo *   Format a HD 3.5" 1.44 Mb diskette in drive A
echo *   Cancel with Ctrl+C or
echo *
pause
format b:
goto stop
:stop
echo *
echo *
echo *   End of formatting service.
echo *
```

## Example 4

The final example is a general formatting program that will format all kinds of diskettes. This was created in a word processor using the copy function as it comprises twelve routines which differ only slightly. Also the help page includes box graphics to make it look nice. Once again the actual necessary program lines are few, less that 25% of the complete program - the rest is cosmetic, a handsome display.

```
echo off
if "%1" == "1" goto form1
if "%1" == "2" goto form2
if "%1" == "3" goto form3
if "%1" == "4" goto form4
if "%1" == "5" goto form5
if "%1" == "6" goto form6
if "%1" == "7" goto form7
if "%1" == "8" goto form8
if "%1" == "9" goto form9
if "%1" == "10" goto form10
if "%1" == "11" goto form11
if "%1" == "12" goto form12
goto help
:help
cls
echo *   GENERAL FORMATTING SERVICE
echo *
echo *   Type one of the following commands, e.g. FMT 3, then press ENTER.
echo *
echo *
echo *                  Diskette to format
echo *
echo *               5.25" 5.25" HD  3.5"   3.5" HD
echo *   Drive type  (360 kb)(1.2 Mb)(720 kb)(1.44 Mb)
echo *
echo *   5.25"    A:  FMT 1     *      *      *

echo *   5.25" HD A:  FMT 2   FMT 3    *      *
echo *
echo *   5.25"    B:  FMT 4     *      *      *
echo *   5.25" HD B:  FMT 5   FMT 6    *      *
```

```
echo *
echo *   3.5"     A:   *      *   FMT 7      *
echo *   3.5" HD  A:   *      *   FMT 8   FMT 9
echo *
echo *   3.5"     B:   *      *   FMT 10     *
echo *   3.5" HD  B:   *      *   FMT 11  FMT 12
echo *
echo *
echo *   To make a system disk add space /s to the command, e.g. FMT 3 /s
echo *   You can also use the /v switch, e.g. FMT 3 /v or FMT /s/v
goto stop
:form1
cls
echo *
echo *   FORMATTING SERVICE
echo *   ====================
echo *
echo *   Format a standard 5.25" 360 kb diskette in drive A
echo *   Cancel with Ctrl+C or
echo *
pause
format a: "%2" "%3"
cls
goto stop
:form2
cls
echo *
echo *   FORMATTING SERVICE
echo *   ====================
echo *
echo *   Format a standard 5.25" 360 kb diskette in high-density drive A
echo *   Cancel with Ctrl+C or
echo *
pause
format a:/4 "%2" "%3"
cls
goto stop
:form3
cls
echo *
echo *   FORMATTING SERVICE
echo *   ====================
echo *
echo *   Format a HD 5.25" 1.2 Mb diskette in high-density drive A
echo *   Cancel with Ctrl+C or
echo *
pause
format a: %2
cls
goto stop
:form4
cls
echo *
echo *   FORMATTING SERVICE
echo *   ====================
echo *
```

```
echo *    Format a standard 5.25" 360 kb diskette in drive B
echo *    Cancel with Ctrl+C or
echo *
pause
format b: "%2" "%3"
cls
goto stop
:form5
cls
echo *
echo *    FORMATTING SERVICE
echo *    ===================
echo *
echo *    Format a standard 5.25" 360 kb diskette in high-density drive B
echo *    Cancel with Ctrl+C or
echo *
pause
format b:/4 "%2" "%3"
cls
goto stop
:form6
cls
echo *
echo *    FORMATTING SERVICE
echo *    ===================
echo *
echo *    Format a HD 5.25" 1.2 Mb diskette in high-density drive B
echo *    Cancel with Ctrl+C or
echo *
pause
format b: "%2" "%3"
cls
goto stop
:form7
cls
echo *
echo *    FORMATTING SERVICE
echo *    ===================
echo *
echo *    Format a standard 3.5" 720 kb diskette in drive A
echo *    Cancel with Ctrl+C or
echo *
pause
format a: "%2" "%3"
cls
goto stop
:form8
cls
echo *
echo *    FORMATTING SERVICE
echo *    ===================
echo *
echo *    Format a standard 3.5" 720 kb diskette in high-density drive A
echo *    Cancel with Ctrl+C or
echo *
pause
```

```
format a:/f:720 "%2" "%3"
cls
goto stop
:form9
cls
echo *
echo *   FORMATTING SERVICE
echo *   ====================
echo *
echo *   Format a HD 3.5" 1.44 Mb diskette in high-density drive A
echo *   Cancel with Ctrl+C or
echo *
pause
format a: %2
cls
goto stop
:form10
cls
echo *
echo *   FORMATTING SERVICE
echo *   ====================
echo *
echo *   Format a standard 3.5" 720 kb diskette in drive B
echo *   Cancel with Ctrl+C or
echo *
pause
format b: "%2" "%3"
cls
goto stop
:form11
cls
echo *
echo *   FORMATTING SERVICE
echo *   ====================
echo *
echo *   Format a standard 3.5" 720 kb diskette in high-density drive B
echo *   Cancel with Ctrl+C or
echo *
pause
format b:/f:720 "%2" "%3"
cls
goto stop
:form12
cls
echo *
echo *   FORMATTING SERVICE
echo *   ====================
echo *
echo *   Format a HD 3.5" 1.44 Mb diskette in high-density drive B
echo *   Cancei with Ctrl+C or
echo *
pause
format b: "%2" "%3"
cls
goto stop
:stop
```

You will notice that the switches /s (create a system diskette) and /v (give the diskette a volume name) can be added to the FMT command. This is done by using the variables %2 and %3 to check for the switches.

## Formatting a hard disk

At some time you may need to format a hard disk. Perhaps you have bought a new one (although they are often pre-formatted), or you want to wipe everything off and start again with an empty disk. As long as you are quite clear that everything you have stored on the disk will disappear this is a simple process, just a matter of giving the format command with the relevant drive letter.

However, there is one major point to remember. If you wish to reformat hard disk C which is usually used to start your computer then watch out. Formatting it will also remove the system files, and you will not be able to re-start your computer without re-installing DOS. To avoid this, you can format a hard disk as a system disk with the /s switch.

Two examples of the format command are:

**format d:**

**format c:/s**

# C. Common DOS Error Messages

When you're working with a computer, things do not always work out as expected: the wrong disk, a forgotten colon, a wrong filename, etc. DOS has a set of error messages to tell you when you've issued an *illegal command.* Don't worry about the command being labelled illegal, all this means is that you've made a minor error in typing it.

This appendix lists the most common error messages, and suggests what you might have done wrong. The error messages are in alphabetical order.

*Note:*
*The actual text of the error message may vary in some cases from that which is shown on your screen. Also, this list is by no means complete. Refer to your DOS manual for information on other messages.*

`Abort, Retry, Ignore, Fail?`

This message is always displayed with a device error message, e.g. a printer or disk drive message. If you know what caused the problem, e.g. diskette upside down or write-protected, then take the necessary action before continuing as follows:

**A**

Aborts the current operation and may even stop the program altogether and return you to the DOS prompt.

**R**

Retry the operation. Select this option if you think you have rectified the problem, or suspect that the problem was only temporary.

**I**

Ignore the operation and pretend that the problem never arose. This will allow the program to continue but may cause many unexpected problems thereafter. It is recommended to try the Fail option rather than this.

**F**

This option was added to DOS 3.3 versions and later. It continues with the program but does inform DOS of the apparent failure.

`Attempted write-protection violation`

The disk you tried to format was write- protected. Change disks or disable the protection by removing the write-protect label from a 5.25" disk or moving the slide position from a 3.5" disk.

`Bad command or file name`

You have typed in a program name or command that doesn't exist in the specified, or current, directory or drive. The computer cannot find what you have typed. Check your spelling.

You may also be able to rectify the problem by extending the PATH command in your AUTOEXEC.BAT file especially if the computer is not finding a certain program or batch file - see chapter on batch files for further explanation of PATH.

`Bad or missing command interpreter`

The file COMMAND.COM cannot be found on the disk that DOS is being started with. You will need to copy this file to the relevant diskette, which for diskette based systems may even involve creating a new system diskette from scratch using your original DOS diskette.

`Cannot load COMMAND.COM, system halted`

DOS tried to re-load the file COMMAND.COM but could do so. Reboot the computer and if the message persists then use a system diskette and copy this file to the relevant disk, which for diskette based systems may even involve creating a new system diskette from scratch using your original DOS diskette.

`Compare error on disk`

DOS has found a difference between two disks you were comparing with the DISKCOMP command.

`Data error reading drive X`

The computer cannot read information from the stated disk. Try typing R to retry a few times. If that doesn't work, then type A for abort.

`Divide overflow`

A program tried to divide by zero or there was an internal logical problem inside the computer. Sometimes this may be caused by a "glitch" (temporary hiccough) in RAM and rebooting the computer will solve the problem although you will loose any unsaved work.

`Drive not ready error`

Normally for diskette drives - DOS is reporting that the drive is not ready for use. The drive may not be properly closed or the diskette may be badly positioned.

`Duplicate filename`

You tried to rename a file but have given it the same name as another existing file, or the specified file cannot be found. Check the file names on the disk, and try again.

`Error in EXE file`

The program file is damaged. The only thing to do is to re-copy or re-install the program.

`File cannot be copied onto itself`

When trying to copy a file you gave the target file (copy) the same name as the source file. Give the copy a different name.

`File creation error`

You tried to write a file but: the directory was full, the disk was full, the original file was a read only file and thus could not be overwritten or the disk is physically damaged. Try removing some other unwanted files to create free space. If a read only file exists with the same filename you cannot write over this file - try giving the file a different filename.

`File not found`

The computer cannot find the file that you specified. Check that you have entered the filename correctly.

`Format failure`

The disk cannot be formatted correctly. It's probably defective.

`General failure error`

Something went wrong but DOS doesn't know what! For diskettes check to see that the drive and diskette types are compatible and that the disk is inserted correctly and the latch closed. Is the diskette properly formatted?

`Illegal device name`

You have specified a device name that does not currently exist in your computer system. Check your typing.

`Incorrect number of parameters`

You specified too many or too few options in the command.

`Insufficient disk space`

The specified disk is full. Erase some files from the disk or try another one. If you get this command frequently on your hard disk, it's time to consider buying a second hard disk or upgrading to a larger one.

`Insufficient memory`

There is not enough memory in your computer to perform the specified operation. This either means that you need more memory (today there's no excuse for having less than 640 kb) or that you're using some memory resident software that has to be unloaded before the particular program you're now trying to use can run.

`Invalid date`

You specified an invalid date in response to the DATE command.

`Invalid directory`

The directory you specified does not exist. Type it again more carefully.

`Invalid drive specification`

The drive you specified doesn't exist.

`Invalid path`

The pathname you specified does not exist.

`Invalid number of parameters`

You specified too many or too few options in the command.

`Invalid parameters`

One or more of the command parameters is wrong.

`Invalid path`

The pathname you specified does not exist.

`Invalid time`

You specified an invalid time in response to the TIME command.

`Non-system disk or disk error. Replace and strike any key when ready`

You tried to start your computer with a non-system disk in drive A. Take the disk out and try again.

`No paper error writing device`

Your printer is out of paper, is not switched on, or is not in the PRINT READY status.

`Read fault error reading drive X`

The computer is unable to read data from the specified drive. This could be a temporary read error caused by your computer. Hit R for retry.

If this happens again, you've somehow damaged your disk and you probably won't be able to recover the data on it unless you can get help with a friend who is very knowledgeable and has the right software. Therefore, go to your back-up disk.

What? You don't have a back-up disk? We warned you this would happen!

---

*Note:*
*If this happens when you're trying to read a disk that wasn't created in your computer, the problem may be that either your disk drive or the disk drive in the other computer is out of alignment. Try reading the disks on the machine on which it was created and/or on other machines. If it can be read on these but not on yours, have a technician check your drive's alignment.*

---

`Target disk is unusable`

The disk you tried to format is defective.

`Target disk is write-protected`

The computer tried to write information on a disk that is write-protected.

`Unable to create directory`

The computer cannot create the specified directory. It may already exist, or you may have specified a name with more than 8 characters or with a space in it.

`Write fault error writing drive X`

The computer was unable to write data to the specified drive. This is usually a computer error. Try R retry. If it happens again the disk may be damaged.

`Write protect error writing drive X`

The computer tried to write information on a disk that is write-protected.

# D. Some Useful DOS Commands

This appendix summarizes some of the most useful DOS commands. Remember that internal commands are readily available from your computer's memory, while external commands require the actual DOS program. This means that disk users will have to insert their DOS disk in the relevant drive to be able to use the command. External commands are marked with a * in the following table.

A similar appendix is also to be found our the earlier book **PC Crash Course and Survival Guide** - this appendix has been revised with several commands being added.

For many commands it is important to note that this appendix only provides a summary of some of the ways to use it. Many commands have other "switches" and uses. Consult your DOS manual for more information on the commands.

The following commands are described:

| | | |
|---|---|---|
| ● | *ASSIGN | Temporarily change the drive name |
| | *BACKUP | Make back-up copy of hard disk content |
| | CD | Change subdirectory |
| | *CHKDSK | Check disk |
| | CLS | Clear screen |
| | COPY | Copy files |
| | DATE | Change the computer's date |
| | DEL | Delete files |
| | DIR | Display list of filenames |
| | *DISKCOMP | Compare disks |
| | *DISKCOPY | Copy disk |
| | *GRAPHICS | Prepare DOS for graphics printouts |
| | *FC | Compares files |
| | *FORMAT | Format disk |
| | *KEYB | Keyboard program |
| | *KEYBUK | Keyboard program |
| | *MODE | Communications/printer port command |

| | |
|---|---|
| *MORE | Displays one screen at a time |
| MD | Create (make) subdirectory |
| PATH | Gives DOS a list of drives/directories to search |
| *PRINT | Printing files with DOS |
| PROMPT | Change prompt |
| *RESTORE | Restore (recopy) files to hard disk |
| RD | Remove (delete) subdirectory |
| TIME | Change the computer's time |
| TYPE | Type the contents of a file |
| *XCOPY | Copies files and subdirectories |

*Note:*
*The examples given in this appendix are just that - examples - and nothing more. You may well have to adapt the commands to suit your own needs.*

## ASSIGN - Temporarily rename a drive

The ASSIGN command allows you to temporarily rename a drive. Try this (if your computer has two diskette drives):

- If you have a diskette based system put your DOS diskette in drive A.
- Type:
  ```
  assign a=b
  ```
- Press the ↵ key.
- Put any diskette with some files on in drive B.
- Type:
  ```
  dir a:
  ```
- Press the ↵ key.

You will notice that the directory of the diskette in drive B is listed despite the fact that you gave the command **dir a:**. In other words the **assign a = b** command has instructed DOS to treat drive B as if it were drive A.

To restore the situation so that A is A and B is B do as follows:

- Type:

  `assign`

- Press the ↵ key.

If you turn off your computer, then the next time you start it the drives will also behave normally, ASSIGN is only a temporary command.

ASSIGN does not work with the FORMAT and DISKCOPY commands.

## BACKUP - Make back-up copy of a hard disk content

This command can be used to make back-up copies of all or some of the files on your hard disk. The back-up copies are made on disks. You can even copy files that would not normally fit onto a single disk (customer files for example). These big files are divided automatically onto a number of disks.

One disadvantage of this command is that the files on the disks cannot be used in the normal way. Instead, they must first be restored (recopied) back into the same subdirectory on the hard disk using the RESTORE command. Moreover, you can encounter problems when you try to restore (using RESTORE) program files that are write-protected. As a result, you should only copy unprotected program files and data files. This command is on your DOS disk (and normally on your hard disk as well).

Before you start, you must have a number of formatted disks available (see section on the FORMAT command in this Appendix). The number you will need depends on how much you wish to copy. You should number the disks starting with 1, and they must be in the proper sequence when you restore the files to the hard disk.

- Insert the first formatted disk in drive A and type one of the following:

| | |
|---|---|
| **back-up c:*.* a:** | This copies all files in the sub-directory in question onto drive A. |
| **back-up c:*.* a:/s** | This copies all files on the hard disk that are in the subdirectory in question and also all files in all lower subdirectories onto drive A. |
| **back-up c:*.* a:/m** | This searches through all of the files on the hard disk in the sub-directory in question, but only copies onto drive A those files that have been changed since the last back-up copying operation. |
| **back-up c:*.dat a:** | This copies all files that end with DAT in the subdirectory in question onto drive A. |
| **back-up c:\word*. dat a:** | This copies all files that end with DAT in the subdirectory named WORD onto drive A. |

**Note:**
*When you restore (recopy) the back-up files, they must be restored to the same subdirectory from which they were copied.*

- Press the ↵ key.

As each disk fills up, you will be prompted to insert the next disk. When the system prompt appears again, copying is finished.

# CD - Change subdirectory

You use this command when you wish to change to another subdirectory. You can change to the desired subdirectory from any other subdirectory.

- Type one of the following:

| | |
|---|---|
| **cd ** | To reach the root directory. |
| **cd \\word** | To change to the specified subdirectory, regardless of which subdirectory you are presently in. |
| **cd \\letters\\quotes** | To change to the QUOTES subdirectory which is found under LETTERS which in turn is found under the root, regardless of which subdirectory you are presently in. |
| **cd ..** | To change to the next higher subdirectory. |

- Press the ↵ key.

When the system prompt appears again, you will have changed to a new subdirectory. To always be able to see which subdirectory you are presently in you should install the PROMPT command in your AUTOEXEC.BAT file.

Subdirectory names must comply with the same rules as those set forth for filenames.

## CHKDSK - Check disk

When you wish to scan a disk for errors or see how much memory is available on it, you can use the CHKDSK command as follows:

- Insert the DOS disk in drive A (not necessary for hard disk owners).
- Insert the disk that is to be checked in drive B.
- Type:

```
chkdsk b:
```

- Press the ↵ key.

The following appears on the screen:

```
Volume xx created Feb 10, 1991 07.20a

     362496 bytes total disk space
          0 bytes in 1 hidden files
     318464 bytes in 40 user files
      44032 bytes available on disk

     655360 bytes total memory
     491136 bytes free
```

CHKDSK can also be used to correct any errors found on a disk - these will be reported if any are found when using the CHKDSK command as indicated above.

- To repair any errors type instead:

  `chkdsk b:/f`

- Press the ↵ key.

Any lost chains (i.e. fragments of files that have got lost) can be saved as separate files which you can then use.

CHKDSK can also be used with a hard disk.

## CLS - Clear screen

This command clears the contents of the screen.

## COPY - Copy files

The COPY command is used to copy specific files that you designate. See also XCOPY for copy subdirectories.

- Insert the source disk containing the files that are to be copied into disk drive A.
- Insert the target disk onto which the files are to be copied into disk drive B.
- Type one of the following:

| | |
|---|---|
| **copy a:*.* b:/v** | This copies all files from disk drive A to disk drive B, and verifies the copies. Verification is called for by specifying /v; this means that after the file is copied, the computer compares the new copy with the original to ensure that they are identical. This adds time to the copying process, but it's well worth it if the file's accuracy is critical. |
| **copy a:*.txt b:/v** | This copies all files having names with extensions of TXT from disk drive A to disk drive B and verifies the copies. |
| **copy a:test.txt b:/v** | This copies the file named TEXT.TXT from disk drive A to disk drive B and verifies the copies. |
| **copy c:\test*.* a:/v** | This copies all files in the TEST subdirectory on hard disk C to disk drive A and verifies the copies. |
| **copy c:\test*.* c:\temp/v** | This copies all files in the TEST subdirectory on hard disk C to the TEMP subdirectory on hard disk C and verifies the copies. |
| **copy a:test.txt prn** | This copies the file named TEST.TXT to the printer. You thus obtain a paper copy of the file (don't forget to make certain that the printer is ONLINE before starting). |

- Press the ↲ key.

When the system prompt appears, copying is completed.

```
1 File(s) copied

A>_
```

# DATE - Change the computer's date

The computer keeps a record of the date. You can change the computer's date as follows:

- Type:

  `date`

- Press the ↵ key.

```
Current date is Thu 01-01-1980
Enter new date (mm-dd-yy):_
```

You have two choices. Either you confirm the displayed date, or you enter an alternative date, i.e the right one. Some programs depend on the computer's date being correct, and this date will also be used when files are saved to record the creation or change date in the disk's directory.

To confirm the displayed date, do the following:

- Press the ↵ key.

To enter a different date, do the following:

- Type in the desired date, putting hyphens between the month and the day, and between the day and the year. For example:

  `08-18-88`

- Press the ↵ key.

# DEL - Delete files

To delete files, you can use the DEL command as follows:

- Insert the disk containing the files you wish to delete into disk drive A or B.
- Type one of the following:

| | |
|---|---|
| **del a:*.*** | This deletes all files from the disk in drive A. |
| **del b:*.*** | This deletes all files from the disk in drive B. |
| **del a:*.txt** | This deletes all files that end in TXT from the disk in drive A. |
| **del a:test.txt** | This deletes the TEST.TXT file from the disk in drive A. |

- Press the ↵ key.

When the system prompt appears again on the screen, deleting is completed.

## DIR - Display list of filenames

When you wish to display a directory containing the names, file sizes, and creation dates and times of all the files on a disk, you can use the DIR command as follows:

- Insert the disk in drive A.
- Type one of the following:

| | |
|---|---|
| **dir** | This displays the information on all of the files on the disk in the default drive. |
| **dir b:** | This displays the information for all of the filenames for drive B. |
| **dir *.txt** | This displays all filenames that end in TXT. |
| **dir c:\test*.txt** | This displays all filenames that end in TXT in the TEST subdirectory on hard disk C. |
| **dir /p** | This displays all filenames, 23 at a time. |

| | |
|---|---|
| **dir /w** | This displays the filenames in five columns, but doesn't include their file sizes or creation dates and times. It's used when you want to get as many file names as possible displayed on a single screen. |

- Press the ↵ key.

## DISKCOMP - Compare disks

You can compare the contents of two disks after you have copied them, useful if you have run DISKCOPY (see below) and wish to check that all went well.

- Insert the DOS disk in disk drive A.
- Type:

  `diskcomp a: b:`
- Press the ↵ key.

The following will appear on the screen:

```
Insert first disk in drive A:  Insert second disk in
drive B:

Strike any key when ready
```

- Insert the first disk in disk drive A.
- Insert the disk that is to be compared with the first disk in disk drive B.
- Press the ↵ key.

When the following appears on the screen, the comparison has shown that the contents of the disks are identical.

```
Disk compare ok

Compare more disks (Y/N)?
```

- Press the **N** key if you wish to conclude comparison.
- Press the **Y** key if you wish to compare other disks.

## DISKCOPY - Copy disk

You can copy the entire content of a disk onto another disk by means of DISKCOPY. The disk onto which you are copying need not be formatted, since this is done automatically by DISKCOPY.

- Insert the DOS disk in disk drive A.
- Type:

  `diskcopy a: b:`
- Press the ↵ key.

The following will appear on your screen:

```
Insert source disk in drive A:
Insert target disk in drive B:

Strike any key when ready _
```

- Insert the disk containing what you wish to copy into disk drive A.
- Insert the disk onto which you wish to copy into disk drive B.
- Press the ↵ key.

When the following appears on your screen, copying has been completed:

```
Copy another (Y/N)?_
```

- Press the **N** key if you wish to conclude copying. Press the **Y** key if you wish to copy another disk.

# FC - Compare files

Compares two files or two groups of files and displays any differences. FC can be particularly useful for combating computer viruses - see **Virus** chapter earlier in this book.

To compare two files, one in the current subdirectory of the hard disk and one on a diskette in drive B, proceed as follows:

- Type:

```
fc myfile.txt b:myfile.txt
```

Note that the two files do not necessarily have to have the same name.

# FORMAT - Format disk

Note that the chapter entitled Diskettes and Drives contains much information on the FORMAT command.

When you wish to prepare (format) a disk for use, proceed as follows:

- Insert the DOS disk into disk drive A.
- Type one of the following:

| | |
|---|---|
| **format b:** | If you wish to format a disk |
| **format b:/s** | If you wish to format a system disk that can be used to start a computer that doesn't have a hard drive. While you can use a system disk to start a computer equipped with a hard drive in an emergency, you usually won't want to do this because none of the instructions in the AUTOEXEC.BAT or CONFIG.SYS file, which are almost always used with hard drive machines, will be available. |

# PRINT - Uses DOS to print files

Prints files via DOS to a printer (not Postscript printers). To print the file MYFILE.TXT give the following command:

```
print myfile.txt
```

To re-direct the printout to a specific printer port type, for example;

```
print myfile.txt /d:com1
```

or

```
print myfile.txt /d:lpt2
```

# PROMPT - Change prompt

You can change the system prompt from the familiar A> or C> if so desired. If you are using a hard disk, there are many advantages to having the system prompt indicate which subdirectory you are in.

- Check that the system prompt appears on the screen.
- Type:

  ```
  prompt $p$g
  ```

  This changes the system prompt so that it presents the current subdirectory.

For example: C:\WORD

- Press the ↵ key.

```
C:>\WORD _
```

It is advisable to insert this command in your AUTOEXEC.BAT so that this type of explicit system prompt will always come up when you start your computer. There are a number of different ways to arrange the system prompt, and they are explained in the DOS manual that came with your computer.

A favourite with a lot of computer hackers is:

```
prompt $t $p$g
```

This changes the system prompt so that it presents both the current subdirectory and the correct time according to your computer's system clock! It's great if you're one of those persons who ends up missing appointments or a normal night's sleep due to spending too much time working on your computer. If you want to be reminded of the date instead of the time, just substitute a "d" for the "t" in the above command.

To intimidate your friends who are afraid of computers, try:

```
prompt WHAT IS YOUR WISH MASTER? $p$g
```

By now you should be able to guess what this will do.

## RD - Remove subdirectory

This command can be used when you wish to delete a subdirectory.

Two conditions must be fulfilled before you can delete a subdirectory, namely:

- The subdirectory must be empty, i.e. it must not contain any files or other subdirectories.
- You must be in the subdirectory on the next higher level, or in the root subdirectory.
- Type:

  ```
  rd test
  ```

  To delete the subdirectory called TEST
- Press the ↵ key.

You have now deleted the subdirectory.

To delete a subdirectory located anywhere in the directory tree, just issue the command, but include the backslash marks and the entire path. For example:

- Type:

```
rd \testscore\history\europe
```

- Press the ↵ key.

## RESTORE - Restore back-up files to hard disk

RESTORE is a DOS command that is usually kept on a hard disk (otherwise, it is on the DOS disk). It is used to restore (recopy) files that have been backed up (copied) using the BACKUP command. The RESTORE command can be used for all types of files that have been backed up by means of the BACKUP command, although files that are writeprotected can cause trouble.

---

*Note:*
*WARNING - if you have any programs that are copyprotected, you must not back them up using BACKUP. Moreover, you must never restore them by means of RESTORE. If you try to do so, they may become unusable.*

---

Before you start, you must have your back-up disks ready, and you must use them in numerical sequence starting with 1. The sequence is important.

---

*Note:*
*Remember that you can only restore files to the subdirectory from which you backed them up.*

---

- Insert the first disk in drive A.
- Type one of the following:

| | |
|---|---|
| restore a: c:*.* | This recopies all files from drive A to the default subdirectory on the hard disk (the subdirectory that you are in). |
| restore a: c:*.*/s | This restores all files from drive A to the default subdirectory on the hard disk together with all the lower subdirectories (from which the files were originally copied). |
| restore a: c:*.*/p | Same as above, but /p causes the computer to *prompt* you, which means that it will ask whether each file that has been changed since you made the back-up copy should be restored to the earlier form on the back-up disk. |
| restore a: c:*.txt | This recopies all files that end with TXT from drive A to the subdirectory on the hard disk from which they were copied. |
| restore a: c:\word*.dat | This restores all files that end in DAT from drive A to the subdirectory named WORD on the hard disk. (You must have copied them originally from WORD.) |

- Press the ↵ key.

You are now asked to insert the first disk, and as soon as it is copied you are asked to insert the next, etc.

When the system prompt appears again, copying is completed.

## TIME - Change the computer's time

The computer keeps track of the current time. You can alter the time as follows:

- Type:

```
time
```

- Press the ↵ key

```
Current time is Wed 08:17:35:26
Enter correct time:_
```

You have two choices, either confirm the shown time, or enter a different time.

To confirm the displayed time, do the following:

- Press the ↵ key.

To enter a new time, do the following:

- Type in the desired time, for example:

```
19:18
```

Note that it is sufficient to give only the hour, and the minutes.

- Press the ↵ key.

The major use for TIME is to be able to display the time as part of your DOS prompt. Also, the creation time of a file is always shown in the directory display.

## TYPE - Type the contents of a file

The type command gives you a way of looking at the contents of a file. TYPE is an internal DOS command and is readily available. The following example assumes that you have a disk in drive A, with the file TEST1.DOC on it.

- Type the following:

```
type a:test1.doc b:
```

- Press the ↵ key.

The contents of the file will be displayed on your screen:

```
Hi there,

This is just one of those boring old example texts.

Bye.
```

To display longer files one screenful at a time use TYPE together with the MORE command as explained under the MORE heading.

## XCOPY - Copies subdirectories

XCOPY copies files and complete subdirectories if they exist. The XCOPY command on its own will only copy files from the current drive/subdirectory.

```
xcopy a: b:
```

The **/s** switch allows non-empty subdirectories to be copied. The **/e** switch allows empty subdirectories to be copied and must be used together with the **/s** switch. Use the following command to copy all directories, including empty directories from a diskette in drive A to a diskette in drive B:

```
xcopy a: b: /s /e
```

# Index

## C



## D

## I



## J



## K



## L



## M

## N



## O



## P

## R

## S



## T



## U



## V

## W



## X



## Y



## Z